ENDORSEME

TERRI GAFFNEY
Spiritual Director and Retired Adjunct Faculty, Seattle University, Seattle, WA

"I have known Helen Goehring since she came to Seattle 20 years ago to serve as a Jesuit Volunteer ElderCorps member. *Transformed by Grief: A Personal History* will be a unique gift for those who are still burdened by the undercurrents of unprocessed grief."

NANCY GRANGER
Director of Mental Health Ministry, St. James Cathedral, Seattle, WA

"I have counseled many people with mental health and addiction issues. *Transformed by Grief: A Personal History* can help them gain insight as to how their life path was influenced by these experiences. One adult parishioner with alcohol addiction had never talked about the trauma of the deaths of his two siblings which occurred early in his life. Such a book is a welcome resource."

REVEREND JOHN HEAGLE
Pastoral & Mental Health Counselor and Author

"Helen Goehring is part of a large caravan of human pilgrims who have not been given the permission, let alone the tools, to carry life-changing losses. *Transformed by Grief: A Personal History* should provide those tools."

KATHLEEN HUGHES, R.S.C.J. (Society of the Sacred Heart)
Theologian and Author, St. Louis, MO

"I have known Helen in her capacity as an Associate of the Religious of the Sacred Heart in Chicago and Seattle. Her deep spirituality is reflected in these essays that underscore that there is no timeline for addressing grief."

Suzanne Lee

Director of Family Ministry, St. James Cathedral, Seattle, WA

"This reflection on one's lifetime losses can provide reassuring context and meaning in preparing readers for their own transitions. To have written this book—her first—at the age of 87 is an achievement in itself and should encourage other seniors to write their stories."

David Joseph Leigh, s.j., PhD

Professor of English, Seattle University, Seattle, WA

"Helen Goehring brings a wisdom and honesty to her experience of grief that is rare in today's culture. This book should be of particular interest to those who suffered early losses that were never addressed."

Mary Lindberg

Chaplain/Lutheran Minister, Columbia Lutheran Home, Seattle, WA

"*Transformed by Grief: A Personal History* provides a valuable resource for anyone processing grief in their own life. I will definitely use this book in my chaplaincy work."

Linda Purdy

UCC Minister, Director of Spiritual Care, Horizon House, Seattle, WA

"Complicated grief makes recovery difficult, especially for seniors who have had multiple losses. *Transformed by Grief: A Personal History* is an ideal resource for those wishing to break grief's isolation and be authors of their own faith by sharing their stories in writing or orally."

TRANSFORMED BY GRIEF

A Personal History

Helen Donnelly Goehring

Transformed by Grief: A Personal History

Designed and printed by Paraclete Multimedia

Printed in the United States of America

First Printing, 2020

DEDICATION

To my mother

Marie Hogan Donnelly

1891–1949

CONTENTS

FOREWORD 11

ACKNOWLEDGMENTS 13

INTRODUCTION 17

PART I *Grieving as a Child*

CHAPTER ONE—*Joanie* 25

CHAPTER TWO—*David* 31

CHAPTER THREE—*Mother* 41

PART II *Grieving for Grownups*

CHAPTER FOUR—*Daddy* 57

CHAPTER FIVE—*Anne* 69

CHAPTER SIX—*Peggy* 83

CHAPTER SEVEN—*Ed* 95

CHAPTER EIGHT—*Steve* 111

CHAPTER NINE—*Miss Mary* 123

CHAPTER TEN—*Rose* 135

CHAPTER ELEVEN—*Jim* 149

CHAPTER TWELVE—*Me* 157

PART III *The Journey Continues*

RESOURCES TO INFORM YOUR OWN STORY

READING RESOURCES 168

INSPIRATIONAL QUOTES
FOR DIALOGUE AND JOURNALING 173

WEBSITES FOR THOSE WHO ARE GRIEVING 178

ARTICLES SHINING A LIGHT ON THE PROCESS 180

PLACE-BASED WRITING RESOURCES 181

THE HEALING POWER OF POETRY AND PRAYER 183

A Summer Day Mary Oliver 183

The Layers Stanley Kunitz 184

The Writer Richard Wilber 186

Gates of Prayer Judaism Prayer Book 187

Face to Face Rabindranath Tagore 188

Aging/Dying Pierre Teilhard de Chardin, S.J. 189

ABOUT THE AUTHOR 191

TRANSFORMED BY GRIEF

FOREWORD

Transformed by Mom

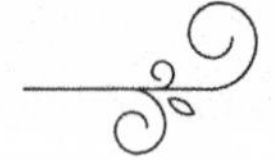

I was eight when I started to hate Mr. Rogers. I'd been neutral about his trolley, loafers, and cardigans for years. But young as I was, I'd never been a fan of death, so the day Mr. Rogers did a show about someone passing away was the day I fully shifted to active disdain. How did he not know I was death-averse?

Now that I'm an adult, years of observation prove I'm far from alone in the sentiment (about death, thankfully, not about Mr. Rogers).

So there's something terrifying and comical at once about Mom asking me to write the foreword of her missive, *Transformed by Grief: A Personal History.* She was around when that whole Mr. Rogers thing took place. Does she not remember? Does she not see the irony?

After all, right now I'm in a Broadway play where the character explores a legacy of familial loss. Right now, I don't want to lose the author of this book—who is 88 herself, having beautifully and resiliently beaten back a range of health challenges. And even though she and I know I'll find wisdom in these pages for years to come, in the exact moments when I myself wrestle with this book's central questions, I will not remember this.

Because this book asks about how we make sense of losing the person we love the most (and who most loves us). This is a conundrum. I'm one of those lucky daughters who's admired my mother for years. She's who I love the most.

This is why there's also something oddly perfect about being asked to write this foreword. Just by thinking about her book's title, I feel transformed by Mom. Ultimately, I *am* glad and relieved to know I and others will have this important collection for years to come. You are holding in your hands a series of graceful essays about being with difficulty, as crafted by the author of my being.

These essays will make you wonder about important things, like whether a present dilemma can be turned into a worthwhile process. Instead of having to untangle grief and love, can they co-exist? Is it maybe even better, if they do? If you wonder these things and come away knowing it's never too late to rewrite what it all means, you'll have gotten the point of these essays. But if you also emerge reminded that there are as many ways to transform grief as there are people who've lost something or someone, Mom's mission is accomplished.

So, I apologize, Mr. Rogers. And I congratulate my mother for wrestling challenge to the ground until connection and tenderness win.

May your own reflections reveal the power of transformation that is ever available to you.

—Kate Marie Goehring, April 10, 2020

ACKNOWLEDGMENTS

So many people and organizations have made this chronicle possible. At the University of Washington, a memoir class taught by gifted writers inspired me to delve more deeply into how I view my life. In his writing class Father David Leigh, S.J., Professor of English at Seattle University, critiqued my essays and encouraged me to "keep writing!" The Seattle Public Library "Seattle Writes" series offered drop-in writing circles that connected me with other aspiring writers. And Hugo House in Seattle was a beacon, offering a writing course that showed me how to get from an idea to the page more quickly.

Certainly, I would be remiss not to acknowledge the parishioners and staff at Seattle's St. James Cathedral, who supported me in my Transformative Power of Grief workshops and whose own healing stories so deeply affected and informed how I think about mine. My writing coach, Lutheran Minister Mary Lindberg, has helped me condense my essays and offer wise direction. Karen Lynn Maher, CEO of LegacyONE Authors, graciously consulted with me about the publishing process and connected me with Debby Mycroft, an excellent editor. Paraclete Multimedia, the designer and printer, took my story from dream to reality by overseeing photos, artwork, and paper selection. Most of all I want to acknowledge my daughter, Katherine Marie Goehring, who has offered her encouragement, direction, creativity, and patience through the entire process. I could not have completed this book—my first—without her engagement.

It definitely takes a team to write and publish a book!

TRANSFORMED BY GRIEF

INTRODUCTION

To lose track of our stories is to be profoundly impoverished, not only humanly, but also spiritually.

—Frederick Buechner

Despite the passing of time, many of us find ourselves grieving the loss of our loved ones long after they have departed. This book explores how people heal from losing those they couldn't have imagined living without.

When I was 83 years old, I began writing this series of essays on deaths that have shaped my life. They capture the illness and death of my former husband from whom I'd been divorced for thirty years. They describe the passing of a gay man, seventeen years my junior, with whom I fell in love during his losing battle with pancreatic cancer. But the deaths holding me hostage the longest were ones that started earliest, from a best friend when I was seven and a boyfriend when I was fourteen, to my mother when I was sixteen. Those were the ones that never seemed to heal.

Who had the resources back then to be present to grief? In the 1940s, adults in my life thought silence was the best medicine for illness and death. With no one to talk to but God, I prayed, cried, and dealt with depression—my own youthful version of Franciscan priest Richard Rohr's contention that "suffering that is not transformed will always be transmitted."

The lack of understanding and the inability to express fear and sadness atrophied my emotional and academic development, as well as my relationships—a high price for not honoring grief.

But a memoir class at the University of Washington convinced me that there is no timeline for expressing grief. My classmates at UW opened the door of my heart as we shared our stories of loss. For me, the most significant death was that of my mother. In the ten years that she was plagued with Parkinson's disease, my family never talked about it despite multiple hospitalizations, the presence of nurses in our home, and the fact that my mother, in her forties, looked and acted as if she was in her eighties. We all pretended she was a healthy woman. To my surprise, the long-buried story elicited tears and gasps from my classmates.

The next week I wrote about my boyfriend, David, and my best friend, Joanie. This exploration revealed that it is never too late to be transformed through grieving; healing begins when we tell the story. Healing does not care how old we are (or aren't) *when* we begin. It just asks *that* we begin. For this reason, I have provided opportunities for readers to journal at the end of each essay.

Writing about grief was new terrain for me and begged answers to questions. Did I know others who carried unresolved grief in their hearts? Did this explain a relative's or friend's depression or need for that extra drink? I saw a window into the lives of my fellow parishioners at St. James Cathedral in Seattle as I watched them approach the Eucharistic table. Who among them is camouflaging a quiet grief? Do they yearn for release from the harsh headwinds that can batter them but don't know where to begin? I needed to know. There was only one way to find out.

With the encouragement of Cathedral staff, I placed an advertisement in the parish bulletin to teach a workshop series on the Transformative Power of Grief. To my surprise, thirteen people appeared in the Sister Mary Rose Room in the Pastoral Care Center for the workshop's first Sunday afternoon presentation. I was recovering from brain surgery and had just learned that I had to move my residence, thanks to my apartment building being sold. But were those reasons to ignore my call to minister to those vulnerable folks? I got my answer as I gazed into the expectant eyes of the people gathered around the table and prayed that I could provide a safe place for them to express their quiet grief. As I focused on them, I felt a surge of physical and spiritual energy.

All the participants felt their grieving had not happened or was incomplete. We established goals, and I outlined a four-week program that included using my essays as a taking-off point for lively, interactive discussions and journaling. One woman who had lost three children read segments of C. S. Lewis's and Frederick Buechner's writings aloud; another displayed the artwork of a boyfriend who died of a drug overdose. All received a list of books and websites on grief. We ended the series with a luncheon prepared by a woman whose little sister died in an accident when she was babysitting her. At the end of this life-giving day, we honored our deceased loved ones as I anointed each participant, and we joined in prayer.

In addition to providing a forum to share stories of loss, the series offered other promising benefits. Friendships blossomed. Two women became roommates; one, in her seventies, was grieving the recent death of her 99-year-old mother, and the other, in her late thirties, was reeling from losing custody of her 8-year-old son. Another woman returned to the church after being a lapsed Catholic for some years. A parishioner who was a long-time supporter of parish bereavement programs stated that she had witnessed growth in each participant: "It is inspiring to hear their stories, and you were honoring them by inviting them to share."

Overall, this book is for an audience who, like me, was not afforded the comfort they craved as they struggled down the lonely road of grief. In the 1940s and 1950s there was little understanding of how a child's grief was distinguished from an adult's grief. Now there are grief support programs in churches, treatment centers, and retirement communities. Hospice is also an excellent resource for families, as well as patients. These groups should find *Transformed by Grief: A Personal History* an opportunity to bring their hearts to healing.

No matter how old you are now—or how young you were when you first lost someone you loved, I invite you to use this book to transform your grief into growth. You've traversed multiple avenues of grieving. You've been to counseling. You've been to grief support groups. You've read "how to" books. Perhaps this is the one that will help you confront the sense of isolation buried inside your heart. This is your story and yours alone.

PART I

GRIEVING AS A CHILD

A child can live with anything as long as he or she is told the truth and is allowed to share with loved ones the natural feelings people have when they are suffering.

—Eda LeShan

"Mom, losing a parent as a child must be isolating," my daughter commented one afternoon as we were walking down the stairs of her New York brownstone.

"Loneliness was built into my childhood due to the deaths I witnessed," I told her. Not only did my mother pass away when I was 16, but also my best friend, Joanie, died in the hospital bed next to me after we had our tonsils removed at age seven. And my first boyfriend, David, burned to death in a family fire when he was 14. The most traumatic loss was my mother's death. Her illness brutally transformed our household, robbing my siblings and me of our childhood and adolescence. After she died, I hoped the sadness would vanish. But it didn't, no matter how hard I prayed and cried.

Hope Edelman, author of *Motherless Daughters,* contends that when a mother dies, a daughter's mourning never completely ends. "It creates a shadow that is hard to brush away, especially when the daughter is caring for her mother during years when she wants to be taken care of." I've never stopped looking for that care provider, but I've learned that I am not alone.

Renowned journalist Elizabeth Farnsworth's mother died of breast cancer when Elizabeth was nine. Her book, *A Train through Time: A Life, Real and Imagined,* conveys how the message of her mother's death was revealed by her father: "We lost mother last night." Farnsworth's reporting from conflicted places in the world was especially meaningful because of the early loss of her mother. "Proximity to her suffering and death made me accept insecurity and also assertively embrace life, which I knew from experience to be fragile," she said. Years later her father apologized for the way he delivered this message, explaining that "Granddad recommended we not tell you she was dying. He thought it would be worse for you to know."

Presbyterian minister Frederich Buechner's father died by suicide when Frederich was nine. Like my mother's Parkinson's, his father's alcoholism and decision to take his own life was the family secret. Buechner recounts his experience in *The Eyes of the Heart: A Memoir of the Lost and Found.* Thank goodness he discovered the power that writing can "make healing and human things happen in a world starving for precisely those things."

As Katy and I walked across town for dinner, I told her that losing a parent as a child *was* depressing and lonely. So was the death of two friends at such a young age. But having this collective experience of sharing our stories—whether with an international journalist or a minister—is a transformative act. It is never too late to grieve. By doing so we are creating our own community, and I find that comforting. I hope you will, too.

CHAPTER ONE

Joanie

And we wept that one so lovely should have a life so brief.
—William Cullen Bryant

On my first day at St. Mary's School in Evanston, Illinois, my mother told Sister Geraldine she'd been concerned about how lonely I seemed. She hoped first grade would help, for I would meet more children and be learning new things.

It was true; I didn't have friends in my neighborhood because there were few children there. My sisters Marie and Peggy were much older than I was, and my brother, Jimmy, who was two years older, teased me a lot and even teased No Name—my doll. "No Name?" he'd smirk. "*Stupid* name." Why did he pick on No Name, my only best friend? But despite these taunts, I knew where to go for comfort. It was in my mother's lap. I would sit on it when we were at church, when Father was driving us home from dining out, and when we were on vacation. When Father showed movie reels from our trips out West, there was always a scene with my face buried in Mother's skirts, my thumb thrust into my mouth.

Most important, she was always by my bedside when I was sick, or with me at the doctor's, when I was getting shots. Somehow, I knew that all would be well if Mother was by my side. But despite knowing where to go for comfort, I still felt that Jimmy's taunts were justified. I was a failure on the playground. I was the last chosen for relay races, three-legged races, and any softball game, and with good reason, for I was a slow runner and poorly coordinated.

There was no soft place to land, until Joanie Smith came into my life. Joanie's family had recently moved into the parish, and Sister Geraldine seated her next to me. Perhaps she knew Joanie was quiet, like me. And like me, she never got into trouble. With curls like sausages that framed her sweet face, she had soft brown eyes that radiated goodness. She looked like one of the paintings of the saints who lined our school's dark oak hallways with the transom windows over each classroom door. She genuflected at the altar with such reverence and serenity. At our First Holy Communion, I thought I saw a halo over her head when she knelt next to me at the altar railing.

Joanie was the youngest in her family, too, and had five brothers. I couldn't imagine five Jimmies, but otherwise, I wanted to be just like her. We'd confide the agony of brothers—a great comfort for me, since I didn't know anyone else who endured that before Joanie. We played hopscotch and jump rope. We passed notes when Sister wasn't looking. Joanie even came to my house after school to play with our dolls and decorate my doll house. But our favorite place was the attic's cedar closet full of Mother's opera gowns and wraps. Joanie would don the maroon velvet, and I the gray satin, taking turns with the long black velvet cape with the white ermine collar. We smelled like mothballs but felt like grand ladies at the opera. Mother never stopped us, delighted as she was to see my lovely playmate and the joy I displayed in being in Joanie's presence. Mother couldn't remember seeing me giggle with such abandon.

One night Mother said Joanie could sleep over. Joanie's mother was concerned that her daughter might get homesick, so I was happy to see how comfortable Joanie felt in my house. Jimmie even played "Go Fish"—my favorite card game—with us. We talked until late, and I pulled out a flashlight so we could read fairy tales under the covers.

That winter Joanie and I missed a lot of school because of frequent sore throats. In the 1930s, doctors were convinced that tonsillectomies were the cure. Our mothers took each of us to a throat doctor who recommended this surgery. I could tell by the questions my mother asked the doctor that she was anxious about the surgery. "Will there be much bleeding? Will she have much pain?" The doctor explained that there was little risk. I would have to eat Jell-O and Junket for a few weeks after the surgery. My throat would feel raw, but then it would get better and better, until I would eventually be able to eat Cracker Jacks at the Varsity Movie Theatre! Our mothers arranged for us to share Room 401 in the pediatric ward at St. Francis Hospital.

The nurses helped us unpack our suitcases stuffed with cards, books, and dolls. Joanie and I played "Joker" and took turns reading *Make Way for Ducklings*. I told her my father's "Pat and Mike" stories passed down from his Irish relatives. We tucked in our dolls, Shirley Temple and No Name, and agreed that we would wear matching pink nightgowns for the next day.

Before I saw the sunlight come through the window, our parents were in Room 401. I was surprised that my father was there for he always went to his office in downtown Chicago early in the morning. My mother pinned a medal on my gown. Jesus was on one side of the medal and Mary on the other. She had one for Joanie, too. Our parents kissed us, and nuns in white habits and veils wheeled our cots down the hall, assuring us in soft voices that Jesus would take care of us while we were on the operating table. "I might be a nurse when I grow up," I told Joanie, waving as her gurney was wheeled past mine. I touched the medal with my other hand.

The next thing I remember is the sorest throat I've ever had. It seemed like it was on fire. Did the doctor leave a lit match in my throat? But when I saw Mother, I knew everything would be all right. Then I went to sleep.

Several hours later I woke up to lots of commotion. Men in white jackets with stethoscopes surrounded Joanie's bed. They pulled the curtains around her bed and wheeled me to another room. My throat hurt too much to ask why Joanie wasn't coming. Her parents and brothers scurried into Room 401, even though visiting hours had already ended. Why were they here so late? I heard the door of Room 401 close. Something was not right with Joanie. But I never imagined she was bleeding to death. Doctors didn't explain to our parents that there was a major artery next to the tonsils. There was a risk of that artery rupturing, and that is what happened to Joanie Smith that day at St. Francis Hospital in Evanston, Illinois.

I don't remember anything between the day I left Room 401 and Joanie's funeral at St. Mary's a week later. At home, my parents wouldn't leave my bedside during the day and hired a nurse for the night, fearing that I would hemorrhage. Not only were they reeling from Mother's recent diagnosis of Parkinson's disease, but they were recovering from the vision of being in Joanie's parents' shoes. They could not bring themselves to go to Joanie's funeral and sent my sister Marie, their oldest child, with me instead.

When that flower-bedecked little coffin went up the aisle, I gasped. Then came Joanie's parents, clinging to each other, and her brothers, who were wiping their eyes with the backs of their hands. My tears soaked Marie's handkerchief and mine. Recognizing that I could not turn off the faucet of tears, Marie took me out of church and sat down on the hard granite church steps, pulling me onto her soft lap. "Don't cry, Helen, honey. Just think how happy Joanie is in heaven." Marie was fifteen. She didn't know what it was like to lose a best and only friend. I didn't want Joanie in heaven; I needed her here to trade notes, jump rope, and dress No Name. I wanted her to dress up in Mother's opera clothes. How could Joanie be happy knowing I was miserable? With no answers, I cried into my pillow at night, clinging to the white pearl rosary girls received at First

Communion. I wondered where Joanie's rosary was. Did she take it up to heaven with her?

Somehow, I felt that if I could talk about Joanie, it would help. But the emotional climate of the times led me to never talk about Joanie again, even with my parents. It's as if her death didn't happen if we didn't talk about it. We wondered, perhaps, if Mother's illness wouldn't worsen, if we didn't mention that either. So, we didn't.

Give sorrow words; the grief that does not speak
whispers the o'er-fraught heart and bids it break.
—William Shakespeare

REFLECTION AND JOURNALING

This was the first death I was to witness in my young life and one of the most impactful, since there was no outlet to experience grief, talk about Joanie, or share memories. If I had, the intense feelings that I brought to bed every night may have come less often, and that would have comforted me.

- Describe the experience of the death of someone close to you when you were a child. Name ways it impacted your life.
- What did others do to comfort you?
- Write about the ways you comforted yourself.
- If you saw a young child who had experienced the death of someone close to them, how would you console that child?

CHAPTER TWO

David

You will lose someone you can't live without, and your heart will be broken. . . . [T]hat hurts when the weather gets cold, but you learn to dance with the limp.

—Anne Lamott

Helen, you are too young to be in love," was my aunt's chant as I emoted about David. He held the door for me. He helped me with my coat. He was *debonair.* When I danced with him at class parties, I imagined that Ginger Rogers must have felt the same while dancing with Fred Astaire. If that isn't love, what is?

David Hurley deserved the Gold Medal for being the most sought-after eighth grader at St. Mary's School. He had wavy red hair, lots of freckles like me, and eyes the color of Lake Michigan when the sun was shining on it. He was fun. He was smart. He was a great dancer. When he asked me to foxtrot at a school dance, I felt that I had won the Oscar. Whether playing ball in Eliot Park, a neighborhood gathering spot, slurping chocolate ice cream sodas at Lyman's Drug Store, or navigating our bikes around the school yard, I was more at ease with David than anyone I knew. When I rode on his bike handlebars, I felt like the Queen of Sheba on Solomon's chariot!

Our favorite times together were at Lee Street Beach, across from my house, where we'd wade in the refreshing waters of Lake Michigan. We wouldn't go far into the water because of the undertows. The previous summer a teenager was caught in one when he dove off the pier, and he drowned. David and I often spoke of that youth, wondering how his family and friends were doing. I didn't want to imagine enduring the loss of a family member or friend. It could have been David or me, for we often dove off that pier. We were more cautious, however, for we knew there was much to anticipate in our lives.

On our walks we'd share our hopes and concerns about high school. David was destined for Loyola Academy, a Jesuit boys' school, and I was going to Marywood School for Girls, run by the Sisters of Providence. I wasn't surprised that David was accepted at Loyola, for he had a combination of gifts that made him an ideal student: academically talented, articulate, and an excellent athlete.

We also discussed our families, including the fact that our mothers were not able to be the mothers that we needed, due to their illnesses, and our fathers were frequently away on business. We were like chicks out of the nest waiting for the adult birds to rescue us, but they weren't there.

Our dads would encounter each other on the Chicago-Northwestern, the commuter train from the North Shore suburbs to downtown Chicago. "Peter Hurley is a grumpy fellow," my father commented at dinner one night. Mr. Hurley had reasons to be grumpy. Mrs. Hurley was in a sanitarium. David was uneasy when he used that word. Years later I learned that the sanitarium was an alcoholism treatment center.

I was surprised and elated when I received an invitation to David's fourteenth birthday party. His mother, who was allowed to come home for this celebration, greeted me at the door. She was as elegant as the antique furnishings in the family's Italianate home. Her red hair was wrapped in a chignon which was the shade of her exquisite gray lace gown. As I was admiring her beauty, she exclaimed, "You're beautiful!" as she gave me a tender hug. I was pleased with her assessment of me, and I silently congratulated myself for choosing the right outfit (a wine taffeta dress with a lace color and puffed sleeves) for the occasion. Mother wasn't feeling well that day; I didn't want to bother her with such trivia as to what to wear to a party. My fashion instincts worked! This was one of the rare good times at David's.

There were other times when he was wrapped in loneliness, as I was. The maid was the one who greeted him when he came home from school. Our maid, Catherine, and my dog, Sandy, were my welcoming committee when I burst through the back door with my arms laden with books. As much as we liked our domestic help, we knew that no one took the place of a mom greeting you with, "How was your day at school, honey?" Instead, I would go up the front stairs and into their bedroom. Mother would be in her chair, head slumped over, and a blue crystal rosary in her trembling right hand. "How was your day, Mother?" I asked. "Did any of your friends come by? Did you hear from Marie?" (Marie, my older sister, was married and lived in Berkeley, California, with her husband and two small children.) While I gave her an injection for the clinical trial, she'd lift her head as if there was a crushing weight on it. "Thanks, honey." I didn't share my day unless it was good news. On one occasion, I was elected to crown Our Blessed Mother at St. Mary's. After I told Mother, her trembling arms embraced me, and I thought she'd never let me go. I was elated by this honor, and her hugs always gave me a surge of spiritual and emotional energy!

Mother insisted that I have a fourteenth birthday party, although my aunts, my father's elderly maiden sisters, said it would be a burden for Mother to have disruptive teens in our home. Surprisingly, my brother, Jim, was my advocate. This bold adolescent shocked my aunts when he told them to "mind your own beeswax!" Jim and Mother won this battle, and with the help of her nurse, Mother tentatively descended our front stairs to greet my friends on that special occasion.

After the guests left, David invited me to walk on Lee Street Beach. While we strolled hand in hand, he slipped a narrow velveteen box out of his pocket with his other hand. It had a silver satin ribbon around it, and inside the satin-lined box was a "slave chain"—an invitation to go steady. The bracelet was sterling silver, engraved "To Helen, From David." My hand trembled as David gingerly wrapped the bracelet around my left wrist. When he hooked the clasp, rather than feeling enslaved, I felt a freedom that was palpable—a freedom to be ourselves with each other; freedom to share our family tensions; freedom to share secrets and know they would remain secrets. It was all I could do to restrain myself from running up to my parents' room to show them David's gift. But I knew that my mother would be exhausted from my party. And I certainly wouldn't tell my father or aunts, for they would admonish me, saying that I was too young to accept such a gift. I never took the slave chain off, even to bathe or sleep. Fortunately, no one asked me what it was. But David and I knew how much it meant to each one of us, and that is all that mattered.

Now that David and I were "enslaved" to each other, we continued our bike rides, walks on the beach, and dancing only with each other at class parties. But our commitment had a short life span. Mother was falling often and spending more time in the hospital. I would sob into my pillow at night, so frightened about what would happen to her and to my family. Sadness and anxiety were my constant companions, even accompanying me to school. I wasn't interested in dances or slumber parties or Wilmette Beach, where all the popular kids hung out. It was just as well, because I had to be home to give Mother her shot in between nurses' shifts.

While my world was shrinking, David's was expanding. He was on the honor roll at Loyola and captured three invitations to Marywood's freshman prom. I did not want him to feel that he had to see only me. Besides, I thought, any hope of our friendship enduring was shipwrecked by my perceived inadequacies. Included among those were the unsettling changes in my body. When somebody called me voluptuous, I went to the Evanston Public Library to look up the word in *Webster's Dictionary.* "Leading to sensual gratification." Did David think I was voluptuous? Of course, I couldn't ask him that! My friends talked to their mothers about their changing bodies, but I couldn't burden my fragile mother with such trifling matters, and Daddy would be embarrassed. And my aunts would be horrified! Sadness and anxiety clamped down on me like a lid on a pot. I would return the bracelet. That way David would be free to date any girl, voluptuous or not.

When I handed him the bracelet after Sunday Mass at St. Mary's, he said that he was sorry that I felt that I had to give it back. I told him that I did not want him to feel tied down to me, especially since we would no longer be in school together. I can't remember what he said after that. But I do remember how naked my wrist seemed with the bracelet gone. That night I sat on the window seat of my bedroom watching the moon appearing like a searchlight on the choppy waters of Lake Michigan, a fog of sadness enveloping me. I felt that a piece of my heart had been shut down. I wish I could tell Mother what I had done and receive her reassurances, but her frail body begged sleep.

Summer was almost over and the kids on David's street were antsy for school. But before school started, the summer ended with a tragedy. Mike O'Brien, a St. Mary's classmate who was considered the class clown, always pushed summer shenanigans to the limit. That fateful day was no exception. With his friends, Dennis Murphy, Joey Campbell and David, they gingerly removed the lid from a gasoline tank to smell the fumes, and Mike foolishly lit a match exclaiming, "Hey, get a load of this. I'm going to drop it in!" That was not his intent, but fate had it otherwise. The burning match cascaded out of Mike's hand and generated an explosion with flames that ascended to the garage rafters.

The horrified boys bolted outside to free themselves from the inferno. Fearing for his father's prized antiques which were going up in flames, David sprinted back into the garage to rescue what he could. Seconds later, what appeared to be Haley's comet shot across the lawn. The boys rolled David in the grass, trying to quench the flames. The maid called the ambulance, which arrived minutes later, taking David's charred body to the burn unit at Evanston Hospital.

I was on my way back from Lee Street Beach after a refreshing swim on that humid August day, when our maid, Catherine, called me to the phone. It was Audrey White, who lived across from David. "Helen, you won't believe what happened!" After receiving the news, I went up to my bedroom, and in my wet bathing suit took my pearl and silver rosary out from under my pillow. This rosary was a gift from St. Mary's School when Joanie and I received our First Holy Communion. As I knelt down and recited the sorrowful mysteries out loud a deluge of tears poured over the beads.

David's mother was confined at the sanitarium, but his father and brothers, Brian and Steven, were by his bedside in the burn unit. My sister Peggy and I had gone to Mass at St. Mary's to pray for David, and when we came home Mother was at the door, trembling Parkinson's arms outstretched. David had died. We held onto each other as the dam burst. "I liked him so much," was all that I could say through my tears. I was afraid to use the word "love," but if I had, she would have understood.

My mind raced with a myriad of questions echoing the disbelief that left me feeling numb. Why did this happen? How could God let the life of this young man with so much promise literally go up in smoke? What was it like for him as he lay in the burn unit with his body wrapped in bandages? Would he have wanted me there, holding his hand?

Life's losses were coming too early and too fast. My best friend in first grade, Joanie Smith, had died next to me when we had our tonsils out. David, my first boyfriend, died a violent death. And then I discovered a note from my Aunt Tess on my father's dresser, saying, "You are doing a fine job of keeping the seriousness of Marie's (my mother's name) illness from the children." Written on her engraved white bond stationery with a St. Louis postmark on the envelope, this was one message unraveling my young life. It seemed that there was a huge magnet dangling from heaven that was yanking all the people I held dear from me. Why get close to anyone if they're going to be the magnet's victim?

I built a wall of isolation around myself as protection from the grief that was pulling me down like the undertows at Lee Street Beach. The day of David's funeral I played sick, for I feared becoming undone, as I did at Joanie's funeral. As I prayed for him from home, I thought of the life David would have had if it were not for that cascading match. Would we have renewed our friendship? He was so handsome; I couldn't help but think what beautiful babies we would have made. But a priest told me that David considered becoming a Jesuit. I could also see him using his intelligence, engaging ways, and sensitivity to inspire and direct the next generation. Grief is more than the loss of an individual, it's a loss of dreams and hopes.

For years I thought I was the only person on earth who had endured losses of such magnitude at such an early age. Then I read a column by spiritual writer Ron Rolheiser, O.M. In the summer of his fourteenth year he lost three people close to him in the small farming community near the Saskatchewan-Alberta border. The summer began with the suicide of a neighbor whose health and body he envied. One night that young man hanged himself. The next week a classmate was killed in an industrial accident, and the summer ended with a friend dying in a horseback riding accident. Rolheiser was the altar server at each of their funerals.

> "My outside world stayed the same, but inside, things were dark, spinning, scary. I was in a free-fall. The specter of death suddenly colored my whole world, and even though I was only 14 years old, I was now an old man inside. A certain youthfulness and *joie de vivre* slipped away from me for good. It truly was a summer of my discontent. I felt myself the saddest 14-year-old in the world. But as all that pain, disillusionment, and loss of self-confidence was seeping into my life, something else was seeping in, too—a deeper faith, a deeper vision of things, an acceptance of my vulnerability and mortality, and a sense of my vocation. I'm a priest today because of that summer, which remains the most painful, insecure, depressed period of my life. But it remains, too, the time of deepest growth. Purgatory on earth. I had it when I was 14."

Like Rolheiser, I had no outlet for my grief. Recently, while purging my files, I unearthed a tattered, yellow clipping from the *Chicago Tribune*, dated July 13, 1947. The headline, "Boy Dies as Human Torch," highlighted that David's father was away on business and that his uncle was Mayor of Chicago. Would this tragedy have happened if Mr. Hurley was in town? Would David have run back to the garage if he knew that his life had more value than his father's antiques? Decades later the "what if's" still plague my grief.

Fifteen years ago, at my sister Peggy's wake in Evanston, I encountered Mike O'Brien's sister. She told me that Mike had died that spring. "In and out of alcoholism treatment," she whispered. What a price he paid for the harsh consequences of that cascading match tossed by an adolescent who merely wanted to show the neighborhood gang what a daredevil he was! I'm still praying for David and his father, the antique collector. I've added the class clown to my list.

As Anne Lamott suggests, losing someone you love is like having a broken leg that never heals perfectly. Every time my arthritis kicks up, I pull out my cane. But that doesn't keep me from dancing! And when I dip, I whisper a thank you to David for teaching me the foxtrot.

REFLECTION AND JOURNALING

As we teach our children to share, walk, and read, so should we teach them to cope with loss and grief, as these are a necessary part of life.

—Maggie Callanan

- Have you lost someone close to you through an accident? Who was that person to you?
- What kind of support did you receive from your family, friends, and spiritual community?
- What was most helpful?
- If you felt alone in your grief, how did you deal with this loss?

CHAPTER THREE

Mother

When a person is born we rejoice, and when they're married we jubilate, but when they die we try to pretend nothing has happened.
—Margaret Mead

How is your mother?" I heard it at school. I heard it at church. I heard it from friends. Like a ventriloquist, I'd push a button that produced a smile and say, "She's fine, thank you."

I knew that I was telling a lie. What people were really saying is that there must be a reason why my mother looked and acted so much older than other moms at St. Mary's School. Her hands shook when she helped serve lunch in the school cafeteria. She shuffled her feet when we shopped at Fountain Square in Evanston. And she often spoke in hushed tones. She had Parkinson's disease, and it would kill her. Everyone seemed to know that but me.

Unbeknownst to me at the time, my mother was diagnosed with Parkinson's when I was six. It wasn't until I was twelve that my father, siblings and other relatives told me she had "neuritis," an inflammatory nerve disease. But no one told me she was going to die. The first inkling I had of the gravity of her illness was when I was helping my sister Peggy pack for Rosemont College, a Catholic woman's college outside of Philadelphia. Although I would miss her terribly, I was excited for Peggy to have the opportunity to go to Rosemont. We were giggling in our efforts to close her suitcase, jammed with Shetland sweaters, plaid skirts, and formals, when there was a knock on the door.

"I'd like to have a word with you," Daddy said. I knew it was something serious, for he never used that expression lightly.

"I want you girls to pray for your mother. She isn't well. It is not as if she's going to die or anything. She just needs your prayers." Before we could respond or ask questions, Daddy left the room.

"She is going to die!" I blurted, tears streaming down my face. Peggy leapt from the suitcase and gave me one of her bear hugs.

"Oh, Helen, honey. Not to worry. She just has neuritis. It is nothing serious. But we must pray for her, nevertheless." I loved my sister, but I didn't believe her when she said Mother's illness wasn't serious. Why would she lie to me? Or did she honestly believe my father?

I'd have to contemplate and process this later, for it was time to drive to Union Station, where Peggy would take the train to Philadelphia. We helped Mother dress and then navigate our stairway while Daddy went out to the garage to get the car. I didn't want to rain on Peggy's parade, for this was to be a time of celebration. But it seemed as if a ribbon of sadness was wrapped around our gray Chrysler as it headed south, along Chicago's Outer Drive. When we arrived at the station, Daddy concluded that the trip down the New York Central track was too long for Mother, so I sat with her on a bench while he took Peggy to her train compartment. When he returned, I was stunned to see Daddy wiping his eyes with his handkerchief. He always seemed to have his emotional faucet turned to "off," but not today. I felt like I was in a funeral procession as we strolled through the station, his arms through Mother's and mine while we walked to our car.

As we drove home along the Outer Drive, it seemed that we were a village of lost souls, not sure of where we wanted to go. One thing was for certain, we didn't want to go back to our home in Evanston without Peggy there. Daddy broke the silence. "The Ringling Estate is having an auction. Why don't we stop by?" The famed circus family had a Gothic manor near our house. The estate had been sold to a developer, and the Ringling family was auctioning its art and antiques. Daddy thought that this sale would be a distraction for Mother and me. It was.

My parents were attracted to a marine painting resembling the view of Lake Michigan from our bedrooms. In it the moon appeared as a searchlight casting its beams over the waves marching toward the shore. Daddy told Mother that he would buy it for her to put over the fireplace in our living room. While he was negotiating the sale, I overheard a conversation between two of Mother's bridge partners. "Doesn't Marie (my mother's name) look terrible? Poor Helen. She has no idea that her mother is dying." That night, sitting on the window seat of Peggy's and my bedroom, I looked at the path the moon cast on the turbulent waters. This was not a painting, but a real-life scene. I needed a life jacket, for I was drowning in a tidal wave of fear. Now I knew why people asked me, "How is your mother?"

My mother was healthy until I turned six. That summer the family went to Estes Park, Colorado—our favorite vacation spot. While we were fishing, horseback riding, and camping, Mother was plagued by balance problems and tremors. We cut our trip short after Daddy telegraphed her doctor in Chicago to make an appointment to see Mother. This was the first of many medical consultations, none of which revealed an explanation for her symptoms. Daddy finally got his answer at Mayo Clinic in Rochester, Minnesota, albeit not the one he wanted. Mother had Parkinson's, a neurological disease which was traced to her having had the flu during the 1918 epidemic, when she was in high school. That epidemic was among the deadliest plagues in human history, killing over 50 million people. My mother could have been one of those 50 million, and although her life was spared, she didn't escape unscathed. The flu planted a virus that exploded in her brain twenty years later in the form of Parkinson's. The doctors at Mayo said there was nothing they could do; she would live ten years. So even though he was privy to the information that my mother's illness was terminal, Daddy did not tell anyone, including Mother. Instead he made up the neuritis story.

Did the presence of neuritis explain why Mr. O'Reilly, the grocery man, would ask me how Mother was when I went to pick up fresh fish on the way home from school? Would that explain why her friends often asked me how she was? Did that explain why my aunts (my father's sisters) came to visit us from St. Louis, thinking they could help Mother? Did that explain why I had to cut up Mother's meat, because her tremors prevented her from doing so? I had so many questions and not enough courage to ask them. The adults acted as if the problem would go away if we didn't talk about it. So, we played the pretend game.

When this charade became too heavy, I would leave the dining room, go up to my bedroom, and release the geyser of tears that had been building up inside of me. To disguise my red, swollen eyes, I'd apply cold compresses to them and return to the dining room for dessert. I fooled everyone but Mother. One night she came up to my room to see why I was gone from the dining room table for so long. When she saw my tear-stained face, she embraced me with her trembling arms and wept into my shoulder.

Despite the gravity, she endeavored to keep her pre-Parkinson's life going. Quivering fingers and all, she helped me with my piano practice. It was "love at first sight" when she accompanied my father for his violin recital in which he played Beethoven's "Moonlight Sonata." Those were the "good" years. As we approached Mayo's ten-year deadline, Mother was forced to give up more. She gave up driving. She gave up gardening. She gave up bridge. She gave up the presidencies of the Catholic Women's

Club and Infant Welfare Society. She and Daddy gave up entertaining and dancing.

Daddy got more help, hiring a laundress, in addition to our live-in maid, Catherine. I tied Mother's shoelaces, addressed her mail, and helped her balance her check book. I spent the summer of my freshman year in high school visiting her at Northwestern Hospital, where I'd see how she was responding to a medication to control tremors. Daddy's office was just a few blocks from the hospital, and he would stop there to visit Mother before we went out to dinner. Over dinner we would talk about everything, except her illness.

As I unroll the scroll of my history, I realize that I bypassed adolescence and took an escalator up to adulthood. I battled depression and yearned for someone with whom to share my feelings. Something in my fourteen-year-old gut told me that there were valuable lessons to learn, things that I couldn't learn from my father. I needed my mother, but she was not able to respond to my anxieties and provide life lessons, as much as she may have yearned to do so. Amidst her outward fragility was an inward nobility. It was her faith that held her together and kept me from falling apart. Her blue crystal rosary was ever-present in her quivering right hand. All these years later, I see that her nobility and faith were her lessons for me.

As her disease progressed and Mother was too weak to come downstairs for dinner, the family would eat in my parents' bedroom. After dinner, we would kneel around Mother's bed, reciting the family rosary. Most of us also went to Mass at St. Mary's Church every morning. Still, no one mentioned her illness. There was an army of nurses: Miss Bosch, Mrs. Green, and Miss Campbell, among a few.

Although I felt that the nurses were intruders in our home, it was actually the disease that was the intruder. In his book *A Grief Observed*, C. S. Lewis, famed Irish journalist and author, confronted his mother's death from cancer when he was ten. "All settled happiness, all that was tranquil and reliable, disappeared from my life." Referring to his younger brother and himself, he commented, "To us boys the real bereavement had happened before our mother died. We lost her gradually as she was gradually withdrawn from our life into the hands of nurses and delirium and morphia, and as our whole existence changed into something alien and menacing, as the house became full of strange smells and midnight noises and sinister conversations. . . ."

It was a similar atmosphere in our home. There were letters, whispers, and overheard conversations amongst the adults. One day I was searching for some bus fare on my father's dresser, where he would empty his pockets of loose change when he came home from work. Next to the change and cuff links was an opened white bond envelope with a St. Louis postmark. The letterhead had an "M" engraved on it for Margaret, my Aunt Tess's formal name. Inside was a note that read: "Of course, the children aren't aware of the seriousness of Marie's illness, and I will never divulge that to them." Another day I overheard Mother's telephone conversation with her friend Marilyn Brown. "Oh, so, so." I knew that was an answer to Mrs. Brown's query, "How are you today?" Mother never complained that she wasn't well. "So, so" was a signal that she was having a bad day.

As I read and heard these secret messages, I'd go to my bedroom and bury my head in the down pillow. Because I was afraid that the laundress, Augusta, might question why the pillow was wet, I kept an iron in my drawer and pressed the pillow slips before I left home for my walk to school. By the time I arrived at St. Mary's, I was floating in a fog. When Sister Donald, my eighth-grade teacher, wrote on my report card that "Helen doesn't pay attention," my parents wondered why. If I had told them that I couldn't focus because I was frightened because of the darkness overtaking our family, they would not have known how to react.

Occasionally I would ride my bike to school and when I did, I would go home for lunch. I relished the time Mother and I would have together. Inevitably, she'd be on the back porch, arms extended. All my worries, whether about misunderstandings with a classmate or struggles with math, seemed to evaporate when she put her quivering arms around me. One day she was not on the porch; she was in the living room with Mrs. Murphy and Catherine. Mother had collapsed at the Evanston Catholic Women's Club meeting. Her face was as gray as her hair; her tremors were worse than ever. When Mother saw me, she assured me she would be fine. I reluctantly returned to school, tears streaming down my face. As my classmates and I were going up the school stairs, I sobbed, "My mother is dying!" Gripping my hand, the Principal, Sister Mary Margaret, called Mother, who assured her that all was well. I was a capricious adolescent, swinging on an emotional pendulum.

As I entered my teen years, I learned that depression was not an acceptable emotion in our household. We always kept a "stiff upper lip," whatever that was supposed to mean. So, I didn't complain when Daddy asked if I could give Mother shots after school between nurses' shifts. That meant passing up going to Cooley's Cupboard in downtown Evanston with my friends to indulge in curly q's (skinny, curly French fries) and Coke. It was probably just as well, for all they talked about was dating. For these reasons I was stunned when my classmates elected me Junior Prom Queen; I suggested a recount. They assured me that I was their choice, so I had to show up. To me, it meant putting on a mask with extra layers of glue, so I could forge a pretend smile.

On prom night I tried to act excited, but this queen was awash in anxiety. Before I went down to greet my date, Jerry, I stopped at my parents' bedroom to say goodnight to Mother. Catherine went in before me to say, "Mrs. Donnelly, Miss Helen looks beautiful and wants to show you her dress." As I leaned over the bars of my mother's hospital bed to kiss her good night, questions raced through my mind: Why is it that my mother is being held hostage to this disease, locked in a cage? My friends' mothers are zipping their daughters into their gowns, greeting their dates, taking their photos, and hugging them before they depart for this supposedly celebratory occasion. Beneath the sheen of my turquoise chiffon dress was the ache of a heavy heart as I descended our staircase to greet Jerry, who was holding a box with a white orchid in it. I pasted on a smile, but I think I was the only prom queen who spent the evening bawling her eyes out in the ladies' room of Chicago's Drake Hotel, with time out to receive a crown of carnations and holly before I danced with Jerry.

The morning my mother died, Peggy, who had married the previous summer and was due to deliver her first child in six weeks, and I attended Mass at St. Mary's. Returning home, as we entered the front hall, we heard my father crying. What a foreign sound that was! I had never heard this man display his feelings so blatantly. It was as if a geyser had burst after all of these years of trying to control his pain. I numbly helped Peggy ascend the front stairs to my parents' bedroom, where my brother, Jim, was standing at the foot of Mother's bed, tears rolling down his face. I had never seen Jim cry, either. The men in our household were showing their vulnerability, while the women took charge. My sister Marie gently pushed Mother's eyes shut. "She had so much to live for!" Daddy blurted. Then we went into our separate bedrooms.

Even though I cried out for it, no one would help me face the reality of Mother's illness or death—the single most significant and painful experience in my life. All I wanted was permission to grieve. I am 87 years old as I write these words, but I still feel like the 16-year-old who was robbed of her childhood and adolescence by the thief of secrecy. My mother's death punctured my childhood, but in the process my character and values were shaped. I learned at an early age that life was short, and we had better use our time here well.

As I open the album of my life, I reflect on what I have learned in the 71 years since my mother's death. I have acquired competence, independence, and strength. It was from my mother that I developed empathy for the vulnerable and downtrodden. Her illness taught me to embrace my own aging and that of others. It prepared me for my work with the vulnerable elderly at Horizon House, a retirement community in Seattle, Washington. Time has dulled the pain enough so that I can view my lost childhood and adolescence with a wider lens, rather than the telescope of years ago, despite tedious detours and lots of false starts.

Rather than view my mother's death with bitterness and loss, blaming my sorrows on the actions of the over-protective adults in my childhood, I prefer to claim it as one of gratitude: gratitude for my children and granddaughters, none of whom my mother knew, but like her, are accomplished, compassionate, and gentle people. Gratitude for my extended family that is there for me when the river of pain is at my doorstep. And mostly, gratitude for my faith, that has seen me through the windstorms of life. By my choosing gratitude, my mother's beautiful legacy lives on through the generations.

REFLECTION AND JOURNALING

When a mother dies too young, something inside her daughter always feels incomplete. There's a missing piece she continues to look for, an emptiness she keeps trying to fill.

—Hope Edelman, *Motherless Daughters*

- Did you experience the death of someone close to you when you were a child or adolescent? If so, what type of support helped you work through your grief?
- If you did not have the help you needed, how did you cope?
- How did the support you received (or didn't receive) affect your choices, habits, or spiritual life?
- Do you grieve differently now as opposed to when you were a child or adolescent?

PART II

GRIEVING FOR GROWNUPS

Only people who are capable of loving strongly can also suffer great sorrow, but this same necessity of loving serves to counteract their grief and heals them.

—Leo Tolstoy

Loss looks different as an adult. In childhood I wasn't taught how to mourn the deaths of loved ones. Through my life experiences dealing with many losses, my views, beliefs, and actions surrounding grief have changed. Most significantly, I have learned that grief has many different facets, and trying to bury the pain doesn't ease the pain.

Determined to avoid replicating the pain I endured as a child, I refused to get into the denial mode. No more pretending that loved ones were not terminally ill. I embraced the reality of death, rather than clutching the past tightly to my chest, but I had some life-giving pauses. This is sometimes easier said than done.

In my twenties, I embarked on a search that should have happened in my teens—discovering what I wanted to do with my life and where to do it. There were many fits and starts, but it was a time that clutched life, rather than death. I left home and plowed new ground in New York City and in San Francisco. I married. I bore three children. I started a Montessori School in Hartford, Connecticut, and went back to school for a Master's degree in Education. But death reintroduced itself when I was in my late thirties. At 4:00 o'clock one morning I had a wakeup call from my brother in Chicago, with the grim news that my father had died of multiple myeloma—cancer of the bone marrow. There was my friend Anne who blocked me from her dark hours of uterine cancer. To help process my pain and grief, I wrote a lament letter to her after the funeral and buried it in New York, where we had spent our twenties together. A few years later, my sister Peggy endured a wretched illness and death from pancreatic cancer.

Another death of a sort introduced itself a decade later. Although I had divorced my husband after eighteen years of marriage, that fact did not prevent me from flying to St. Petersburg, Florida, from Seattle, Washington, to spend his last days with him twenty years after our divorce. I'm so glad I responded to God's tap on the shoulder, inviting me to erase the pain and anger of our divorce. The next year my friend Steve, a gay man with whom I had fallen in love, was felled by pancreatic cancer.

And there was Mary, a resident of the Seattle retirement community where I worked. She and her husband, George, were members of the Greatest Generation—those who lived through the Great Depression and World War II. People born in that generation were resilient and resourceful. Not only had she lost her husband, but also their daughter Marion had died of cancer just months before George passed away. Her remaining daughter, DeDe, and I forged a deep friendship. Today DeDe is among my dearest friends.

Then there was my next-door neighbor Rose, to whom I read the *New York Times* when she was going blind. In turn, she would critique my essays as I read them to her.

The death that took me and many family and friends by surprise was that of my brother, Jim, who died of heart failure in his sleep on Easter Sunday while on a family vacation in Hawaii. At the time I was undergoing a heart procedure in a Seattle hospital. Though I was stunned, as family and friends were, I knew this is the way Jim would have wanted to go. But many of us wished we had had time for a final farewell, as we had had with other loved ones.

During those goodbyes, we held hands, told stories, read poetry, played music, chanted the psalms, and wrote or told our stories. In partnership with loved ones, I embraced the certainty of death, rather than clutching past losses and ignoring the inevitable.

Not only were these activities therapeutic, but also they helped soften the pain of other deaths I had witnessed. Mary reminded me of my mother; it's as if my time with her pulled back the curtain of grief that had been drawn much of my lifetime. The tales of how she and George met, their love of music and art, and the elegant gowns she wore to embassy parties, lifted my spirits. Rose's thoughtful listening helped erase the pain of my divorce. And Steve's illness and death were an occasion for creating community. From these treasured souls with whom I traversed the valley of mourning I learned that I did not need to give the sadness of life the power to define me. Following are tales of compassionate presence with those whom I accompanied during their last days. They continue to occupy large chunks of my heart, and yet there is still space for the others who I know will follow. I think Tolstoy was right on the mark when he said that love is the answer when we are confronting grief.

Throughout my lifelong journey of embracing grief, it was my focus on hope and deepened spirituality that was truly transformative. Prayer, regular sessions with my spiritual director, and daily Mass all contributed to that foundation. Outreach to the mentally ill, the incarcerated, and the poor has also been a cornerstone of my healing. In the final chapter, "Me," I describe how I am now prepared to embrace my own passing with the nobility of my mother, and with open, heartfelt conversations with my loved ones.

CHAPTER FOUR

Daddy

There is no grief like the grief which does not speak.
—Henry Wadsworth Longfellow

I was rummaging through my healthcare files in my Seattle condo when I unearthed a wrinkled, beige sheet marked, "Autopsy–James Leonard Donnelly–October 4, 1972." In his final years my father battled numerous diseases. He had multiple myeloma—cancer of the bone marrow. He had atrial fibrillation. He had kidney disease. I had no idea that he had this mixed bag of health challenges!

Until Daddy began having backaches, my siblings and I thought he was invincible. At 74, he was still running the Illinois Manufacturers' Association (IMA) after forty years at the helm. He sat on corporate and nonprofit boards. His phone rang off the hook with invitations from widows.

It wasn't always that way with my father. When he was in his forties, and I was young, his heart was tied up in knots with the secret of my mother's terminal illness. It took energy to disguise that she was so ill with Parkinson's disease, which dragged on for ten years. This transition from caring for a sick wife was awash with adjustments for everyone in the family.

One such adjustment that came after Mother's passing was a shift in our living space. I was aghast when my father told me that he would be switching bedrooms with me. The idea was for me to move into the master bedroom suite that was home to my parents for over twenty years. In a sense, it was the upstairs living room, for when my mother was no longer able to come down for meals, we would have dinner in their room, which had a fireplace, a chaise lounge, and a window seat with a view of Lake Michigan. Now Daddy would inherit my bedroom in the back of the house. Why would he forfeit this piece of high-end real estate for my relatively modest space? Perhaps this decision was also because he had been brought low by ten years of relentless affliction. Sleeping in the room that he shared with his wife for twenty years would serve as a constant reminder of what he had lost. Did this shift in his living accommodations help him heal? What did that healing involve? Did he cry himself to sleep the way I did? It was hard to tell with Daddy. He kept his feelings close to his chest, just like a hand of cards that he didn't want to reveal to his bridge partners.

Perhaps the weight of my mother's illness had finally lifted for Daddy. He no longer had to rush home to hold her hand, trying to comfort her. He no more had to juggle nurses' schedules and coordinate them with my routine. Despite his Herculean efforts, there was nothing more for him to do to bring about a cure or at least some relief from the tremors, the falls, and the depression. No more calls to doctors and no more research at the Crerar Medical Library at the University of Chicago, where he would go at lunch time. I thought of the moth as it emerges from the cocoon, when going through a metamorphosis. Daddy left the cocoon of Mother's illness and death, and immersed himself in his work, politics, and social life.

But for me, Mother's illness and death were burdens that I carried around like that of Sisyphus. Daddy never asked me how I was doing. But he sent me to modeling school, so I would acquire poise, and to Northwestern Drama School for elocution lessons to "gain confidence in myself." As I reflect on this time, I realize that he wanted me to hold my own in the circles in which he navigated. Those opportunities served me well in my professional and social life. They also comprised generosity with a capital "G." To Daddy, generosity was a reflection of love with a capital "L."

Daddy breathed a sigh of relief when I married in Chicago and settled there, rather than on the East or West Coasts, where I had spent much of my twenties. But he was devastated when Ed, my husband, was transferred from Chicago to Hartford, Connecticut, for a new job opportunity. Daddy loved our son Eddy, just one year old. Now that Eddy had a little brother, Tommy, who was born a year later, Daddy was looking forward to seeing his grandsons grow up. Nevertheless, he traveled to Hartford at least once a year. A non-flyer, he would take the train from Chicago or drive with his friends the Brandons. He even made a special trip for our daughter Katy's baptism and was often there for their birthdays. The children and I always looked forward to his visits, for he brought a light touch to our household.

There wasn't much laughter in our Connecticut home. It seemed that Ed and I couldn't agree on lots of things–the schools the children attended, how we spent our money, and where we lived. But when Daddy visited, there was an aura of lightheartedness and a sense of celebration. He took the boys fishing at our town dock. He played ball with them and read them stories. One night Daddy planted rubber alligators and weird noise boxes in their beds. They retaliated by short-sheeting the perpetrator's sheets. Daddy never let on to these pranks when he came down for breakfast the next morning.

The fun times with Grampy—as the kids called him—weren't limited to visits to our home in Connecticut. There were treks to New York City with the children. Those included forays to the dinosaur exhibit at the Museum of Natural History. When they were older, we would go to the Christmas Show at Radio City Music Hall and ice skating in Central Park. The favorite of all was lunch at the English Cafe at Rockefeller Center's ice-skating rink.

One Thanksgiving weekend, he took me to Bergdorf Goodman's on Fifth Avenue, where he helped me select a leopard coat.

There were also more sober moments. Our son Tom was struggling in school because he had Attention Deficit Disorder. His first-grade teacher was unsympathetic and kept him in from recess or held him hostage after school, rather than accepting this as a normal condition for many little boys. I was determined to remove Tom from this destructive situation and found a private school that would be much more suitable. Because we did not have the funds to pay the tuition, I asked Daddy to help. The week after a visit to Connecticut, I found a check in the mail to cover a year's tuition at this school. With a class of ten, as opposed to thirty, and a grandmotherly teacher with a kind manner, this was an investment that brought huge dividends for Tom.

Our children were among three of my father's twenty-one grandchildren. My sisters Marie and Peggy each had eight children; my brother, Jim, and his wife, Charlie, had two. For Daddy's grandchildren to forge bonds with him and each other was tantamount to him leaving his footprints in the sand. There were few opportunities to do that since we were scattered all over the country. To rectify that, he rented a house in nearby Groton Long Point on Connecticut's Shore for the month of August. This decision accomplished just what my father had hoped. The cousins frolicked on the beach, played tennis and volleyball, fished for flounder, and sailed on Long Island Sound.

But the visits with Daddy were fewer and fewer. He was losing energy. Most concerning were his backaches, which began when he went to the Chicago O'Hare airport to pick up a business associate. When he lifted the gentleman's suitcase into his car, it was as if a bolt of lightning had charged through my father's spine. I could tell by the tone of his voice during my weekly calls to him that he was discouraged, for there didn't seem to be any relief for his back pain. Arthritis ran in our family. His sisters were almost crippled with it. Even his daughters were arthritic. So his doctor assumed the source of his pain came from his joints, and he treated him with steroid injections and gave him a prescription for physical therapy. Daddy even went to a chiropractor and masseuse. Nothing helped, not even the pain medication. His voice diminished to a whisper, disguising the strong, self-confident and vigorous man I knew. According to my sister and brother in Chicago, he was increasingly gaunt. Daddy did not need to lose weight. He was a tall, lean man, proud of the fact that the clothes he wore in law school still fit him.

Concerned by this deterioration, my brother, who lived in the Chicago area, contacted his golf partner, John Gordon, for a second opinion. As soon as Dr. Gordon saw Daddy, with his pale face, fragile skeleton, and sunken eyes, he admitted him to Evanston Hospital for tests. A bone marrow biopsy revealed cancer cells. That meant that he had multiple myeloma—cancer of the bone marrow. The major symptom was bone pain, due to compression fractures. No wonder he was so miserable! I immediately hired a babysitter and flew to Chicago.

When I walked into Room 207 of Evanston Hospital, I thought I had made a wrong turn down the hospital corridor. The man propped up in the bed was a mere skeleton compared to the energetic man I called Daddy. He was so anemic that the doctor ordered a blood transfusion. And his heart was failing. My father had been transformed from a self-possessed man, an always-in-charge fellow, into a feeble, vulnerable one. Despite his fragility, he was nobody's fool. Standing by his bedside soon after the transfusion, I gazed at a man facing his mortality, and he was terrified. He expressed his fear by complaining about the doctors. He proclaimed that they didn't know the first thing about medicine. That's when I started mourning Daddy's demise. I had experienced enough grief by now to understand that grief begins before physical loss occurs.

But there were a few moments of levity. As was his custom, when Daddy came home from work, he often poured himself some Cutty Sark—his favorite Scotch. The family would gather around him, as he stretched out on the chaise lounge in the master bedroom and told us about the battles with labor unions and advocates of the Taft-Hartley law. That "libation" was just enough to help him unwind.

Bill, an old friend and member of the Illinois Manufacturers' Association board, was across the hall from Daddy's hospital room, where he was recovering from a stroke. Every night around 6:00 p.m., Daddy's nurse would wheel him to Bill's room. After the nurse left, Bill would open the drawer of his bedside table, pull out his flask, and pour them each a shot of his favorite Scotch blend whiskey. Then they would reminisce about the "good old days," especially golf tournaments, days at the racetrack, and their favorite subject–politics. I think those visits added a few months to Daddy's life.

Aside from those moments of lightheartedness, all I could think of doing was to hold his fragile hand and say the rosary. I reflected on the times, 25 years ago, that our family would kneel around my mother's bed in my parents' bedroom, reciting the rosary. We were begging Mary to plead a case with her Son to save our dear mother. We were just kids, and we needed her. The thought of enduring the turmoil of adolescence without our mom was terrifying.

Now it was our turn to pray for and minister to Daddy. I gathered with family and friends as they held vigils at my father's bedside, taking turns praying, wiping his brow, and holding his hand. My sister Marie and I took turns making trips every month. I found comfort in knowing that my brother, Jim, and sister Peggy lived near Daddy.

Difficult though it was to leave Daddy's bedside as he was coming to the end of his life, I had two jobs awaiting me in Connecticut. One was as a teacher in the Groton Public Schools, and another as a parent of three children, ages seven, nine, and ten. When I left Daddy's bedside to depart for Connecticut, I kissed him on the forehead, telling him that I loved him, and that I'd be back in a few weeks. Once back home, I called him every night in the hospital, although he was often too weak to talk.

I was scheduled to leave for Chicago in a few days and had already lined up a neighbor to pick up the children after school. Ed would be there at night to give them dinner. It was a restless night, and I finally fell asleep at 1:00 a.m. At 4:00 a.m. the phone rang. "Who in his right mind would call at this hour? Everyone knows how I cherish my sleep! It's probably the wrong number," I mused. I rolled over to the nightstand, sheets wrapped around me like a sarong, and grabbed the phone, hoping it wouldn't wake up the children.

"Hello." I murmured in my grumpy half-slumber.

"He's gone."

It was Jim calling from Chicago. My father had died a half hour before at Evanston Hospital, a mile from where I had grown up. Multiple myeloma and a heart attack were the culprits.

"I was going to wait until you were awake, but then I thought you'd want to know right away," blurted Jim.

The truth is, Jim, my only brother, and my father's namesake, needed to be comforted by his little sister. I can't remember what he said, except when the wake and funeral would be. I felt an equal urge to be comforted and announced my father's passing to the entire household that was sleeping.

"Grampy's dead!" I bellowed. Our sleepy-eyed children came dashing into our bedroom. They knew that their grandfather was coming to the end of his life, but they had never lost anyone close to them. They didn't know what death was like, but they were smart enough to know that life would not be the same without their grandfather, and we'd miss out on a lot of fun. My siblings and I were now the oldest generation. I had lost my advocate and support system.

When I walked into Donnellan's Funeral Home for Daddy's wake, I was especially touched by the emotional responses of my teenaged nieces and nephews, who sobbed when they saw their grandfather laid out in the casket. They had a long history with their Grampy, who dressed up as Santa every year, attended all their birthdays and graduations, and taught them how to play golf. At the wake I was greeted by throngs of people from all walks of life standing in line to pay their respects. My high school and college friends were there. Mayor Richard Daly Sr. was there. Our former gardener, cleaning lady, and laundress were there. Daddy had been good to all of them. Katy, age seven, knelt on the *prie-dieu* (prayer kneeler) and said a few private words. I'm sure that whatever her words were, her Grampy (and God) cherished them. To this day, as a Prayer Partner for Unity Church in New York, she calls in prayers when I or a friend are enduring a health or a work challenge. Her brothers served as altar boys for the funeral Mass. I was so proud of them in their red cassocks and white surplices. They were reverent, respectful, and solemn—all appropriate emotions for the liturgy.

At the reception afterwards, my high school friends wistfully shared memories of the jokes Daddy told at the dinner table, and how he loved to dance and play the violin. "There was never a wallflower in the room when your dad was there," said one of my high school pals. This was clearly a man who helped others smile, laugh, and feel good. Quite a legacy. The Illinois Manufacturers' Association passed a resolution that referred to Daddy's energy, wisdom, and executive ability. The most significant and poignant accolade was the reference to his "great personal charm and warm regard for people that won him a host of friends."

Daddy always managed to claim center stage–he was handsome, articulate, and charming. Some of his friends and colleagues referred to him as "Mr. Ambassador." He looked and acted like one. He was also the consummate storyteller, always having an old yarn, a prank, or a joke up his sleeve. Now the final curtain was drawn.

I managed well at the wake and funeral, where I was surrounded by family and friends. The true test was when I returned to Connecticut, where I was expected to act as if nothing had changed. One day I had a particularly hard time with my unruly class of eighth graders. They were non-readers and understandably angry at having been passed from grade to grade without anyone recognizing their learning disabilities or taking the time to teach them their vowel sounds. Usually I was quite patient with them, but on this day I "lost it" and cried. I told them that my father had died, and that I was very sad. They did not understand, for most of them did not have caring fathers. They were basically orphans of society, living in Quonset huts outside the Groton submarine base, with their fathers out at sea for months at a time.

News of my episode of tears traversed up and down the school hallways. "We got Mrs. Goehring to cry in our class," echoed, as if it was a triumph. The principal called me to his office, saying that I should never display that kind of weakness in the school. Yet, routinely, he and his staff members shouted at students for the least infraction, such as talking in the hall, until they cried. In contrast, another day, my dear cleaning lady, Maria, was scrubbing the kitchen floor. I was at the dining room table correcting English compositions, and I burst into tears. She put her arms around me and patted me on the back as I hugged her.

"I miss him so much. Life will never be the same," I sobbed.

"It is good that you are crying. We need to mourn those who we loved," she replied.

I was grateful for her empathy and understanding. She was a single mom who was hanging on by her fingernails to every bit of security she could muster for herself and her two-year-old son. I was also comforted by a call from my friend and neighbor Mary Thompson, asking if she could visit. She appeared at my doorstep, a bouquet of autumn flowers in hand, inviting me to tell stories of my father. It was a comforting moment.

Now at 87, I reflect on the many things my father taught me—things that very few women of my generation were exposed to. He took me to Congressional Committee hearings, explaining that this was the heart of passing legislation favorable to his members. For my high school graduation, he presented me with a grand tour of Europe. When I had my first job out of college, working for a Chicago lawyer, we'd debate the difference between the Circuit Court and Superior Court, and a misdemeanor and a felony. He taught me how to interact with his business associates. These experiences fostered in me a fascination with politics and helped me acquire skills that have served me in my career in philanthropy, especially liaising with boards and major donors.

Recently, when I was sorting through memorabilia as I downsized to a smaller apartment, I unearthed a tattered holy card buried in a prayer book. This was the memorial card distributed at Daddy's wake and funeral, forty years ago. Written by the German Jesuit Alfred Delp, it read:

"When through one man a little more love and goodness, a little more light and truth come into the world, then that man's life has had meaning."

It still serves as a reminder of how blessed I was to have a father who went about doing good and bringing light and truth into the world. One couldn't ask for better reviews than that!

REFLECTION AND JOURNALING

Grieving is a journey that teaches us how to love in a new way now that our loved one is no longer with us.

—Tom Attig, *The Heart of Grief*

- Why do you think my father found it difficult to comfort me after my mother's death?
- Share an experience of someone close to you who did not understand why you were grieving the loss of someone who was so important in your life.
- What are some of the things that others did or said that were helpful?
- Some people, such as the school principal, expect us to hide our grief. Others are open and sympathetic. Do you believe there are situations where we need to set our grief aside and control our emotions?

CHAPTER FIVE

Anne

My friends are my "estate." Forgive me then the avarice to hoard them.
—Emily Dickinson

I was lying on my back with ice packs tucked under my spine. This was one of the worst spinal stenosis flare-ups I've had in years. The phone rang. My back ached too much for me to pull myself up to grab the receiver, so I yanked the telephone cord. The phone tumbled off the table and on to my belly. It was Anne calling.

"Helen, I'm just come from the doctor's office. I may have cancer!"

My back pain paled in comparison to the message that came over the wires. This message not only provoked a back spasm, but it also shut down a piece of my heart as I took in its implications. I could hear the absolute terror in her voice. Anne, whose *modus operandi* was the epitome of calm and composure, was in a state of disbelief that such a verdict should be handed down to her.

This verdict was no surprise to me as I rehearsed our recent conversations. One of my closest friends ever, Anne had displayed signs of a serious illness for months. At our weekly dinners on Chicago's Near North Side, she would tell me of her fatigue as she played with her favorite salmon dish without the fork ever entering her mouth. Her usually vibrant expression was now that of deep concern etched over a gray complexion. Her brown eyes were sinking deeper into her finely chiseled face. And there was less and less of her already scant body. At those dinners I would chant imploringly, "Annie, don't you think you should check in with the doctor?" "Oh, no," she replied. "I'm just working too hard. When I retire, I'll feel better."

Anne was a social worker at Catholic Charities of Chicago. Even though we were native Chicagoans, we met in New York City, where we moved after college. We became opera and theatre mates, double-dated, museum-hopped and went to daily Mass together. Although we both loved New York, eventually our job opportunities brought us back to Chicago. Anne was invited by Catholic Charities to help resettle Vietnamese immigrants in the city. I had received an offer to be Development Director at Barat College of the Sacred Heart, my *alma mater* in Lake Forest, outside of Chicago. One of the reasons I was so pleased about this move was the fact that Anne and I could renew our friendship.

In addition to the attractive job offer, I think Anne was lured back to Chicago by her dear friend Ron—a wonderful fellow who was smitten with her. They lived in the same apartment building off Michigan Avenue. He was about to retire as Dean of the Business School at a Chicago university. Then they would move to Florida, where they intended to marry.

They were Shakespeare buffs, and every year they ventured to Stratford's Shakespeare Festival. But this most recent trip proved to be anything but celebratory. They had just come back to their Bed and Breakfast after a performance of *Measure for Measure* when Anne began hemorrhaging. Ron wanted to take her to the hospital. She tried to push his concern away, for she did not want to rain on this long-anticipated trip. Anne promised to see a doctor when they returned to Chicago. When I received the call, she had just returned from her appointment at Northwestern Medical Center. The doctor told her that pathology reports revealed cancer cells. She needed a hysterectomy to remove the cancerous uterus, and he scheduled the surgery for the next week. She said that Ron would let me know the outcome.

I stormed heaven, telling God that there were so many of us who wanted to keep Anne here on earth for at least a few more years. At the same time, questions were ricocheting through my head as to why she had postponed seeing the doctor. I was also dismayed by Ron's lack of communication. It had been a week since the surgery. Then one day after Mass I had a voicemail: "She's recovering nicely but she may need some chemotherapy and radiation. We'll let you know how it goes."

That's the last I heard from Ron. My heart sank even deeper. Anne did not want calls. She did not want visitors. She did not want flowers. Like my parents in their attitude toward illness, she seemed to think that her disease would go away if no one acknowledged it. The fact that she needed treatment meant that the cancer was spreading. I heard murmurings and whisperings from her friends and colleagues, just as I did when my mother was dying. But I refused to hang black crepe over Anne. Then one night she called me.

"Helen, I have just come from visiting Cardinal Bernardin. It was the most amazing experience. I felt that I was in the company of a saint. He was such a comfort." What a change in tone from Anne's last call, when she told me of the cancer. Her voice was calm and hopeful.

Joseph Cardinal Bernardin, the Archbishop of the Catholic Archdiocese of Chicago, was recovering from surgery for pancreatic cancer. While a patient at Loyola University Hospital, he visited other patients, becoming the "unofficial chaplain" to Chicago cancer patients. When he attended the wakes of those who had died from cancer or other tragic circumstances, people slipped him notes with the names of friends and relatives suffering from cancer. He wrote letters. He made calls. And he invited some of these fragile folks to visit him. Anne was one.

The Cardinal was waiting for Anne when she rang his doorbell. He invited her into his parlor, and they sat in front of his fireplace for an hour, sharing their stories. They cried. They prayed. They comforted one another. And he blessed her. She sounded like her old self, and I felt a glimmer of hope. That was the last time I spoke to her.

A month later I ran into Anne's friend Patsy at the Women's University Club. She told me that Anne needed our prayers. She had heard this from Ron. My heart sank. That sense of peril that I heard in Ron's voice when he called me with the prognosis returned. I knew that he would be by her bedside, but Anne would not allow anyone else to be there, not even a priest. (One day the pastor of Holy Name Cathedral went to her apartment. Ignoring the concierge's orders to turn away all visitors, he went up to Anne's apartment to give her a final blessing.)

I was on my way to Mass when my friend Jean called. Jean was Anne's cousin and my former roommate in New York. She had introduced me to Anne. That started a friendship that was one of the deepest I've ever had. Now Jean was married and living in the suburbs.

"Helen, do you remember Anne Templeton? "

"Of course, I remember her. She's one of my best friends!"

"She died today."

I exploded in disbelief! Jean did not realize how close Anne and I were. She and her husband were out of touch with what was going on in the city. As Anne's cousin, she was simply being a dutiful relative and making a call that no one wanted to receive. She apologized, saying that someone else should have called me. I hung up, sobbing.

I called my sisters and wept. I called my friends Tom Graham and Jim Hayes and wept. When I called my daughter, Katy, she bolted over to my apartment and swept me into her arms as I turned on the fountain of grief. She filled my bathtub with warm water, adding her home-made lavender bath salts. She put on my favorite meditation tapes, placed my pink spa pillow under my neck, and let me soak the grief out. Then she wrapped me in my terry cloth robe and tucked me into bed, so I could take a much-needed nap. The healing process had commenced.

Katy went to Anne's funeral with me. My sisters would have come, but they were away on vacation. There were lots of Anne's friends there, including Tom and Jim.

Three priests were celebrants, and Father Egan, the priest who went up to her apartment to bless her, gave the eulogy. He believed that this was the moment God wanted Anne. Ron would not have agreed, walking behind that casket with fists clinched and tears streaming down his face. I was angry at Anne for tuning him out, too, when he urged her to go to the doctor.

In the eulogy Father Egan spoke of the diversity of the mourners. I thought I knew so much about Anne, but I learned a lot more at that funeral. She really spent most of her time listening to other people, not talking about herself.

One day after Anne's passing, Ron invited me up to her apartment. He had something to give me. When I entered the apartment, it was difficult not to show my shock as to the condition of her once charming home. Her white carpeting was covered with stains. There was an oxygen tank in the corner, next to her eighteenth-century cupboard. There were bottles of pills, a hot water bottle and towels on the mahogany dining room table. It never occurred to me that Anne would be on oxygen or taking all of those pain medications. No wonder she didn't want any of her friends to see her! Amidst her humility, she was also proud. And rightfully so. She was a beautiful woman. She broke many hearts, but none were more broken than Ron's.

Ron told me that Anne had left me something in her will. Then he handed me a white cardboard box with a plate wrapped in green felt. It was an antique sterling silver platter with an engraved "T" on it. I teared up as

I clutched it against my chest. Oh, my, with all she had going on, she took time to figure out what I wanted of hers. Then he took me to her closet and asked me to help myself. Her wardrobe was there in all of its splendor. The closet was filled with designer jackets, lovely gowns, exquisite scarves, and dozens of shoes. I never thought of Anne as being a clothes horse, but she always dressed appropriately for the occasion. I told Ron how hard it had been for me to not be in touch with her, and he said that she could not bear to have her healthy friends visit her, knowing that she would never see them again.

I did not want to carry around this sense of lovely times lost like an albatross, so I made an appointment with Father Bill Moriarity, associate pastor at Holy Name Cathedral. Anne was a parishioner there, and he was a celebrant at her funeral. He also knew me in his role as chaplain at Northwestern Medical Center, when I was a patient in the cardiac unit. Father Bill was a kind-hearted and compassionate man who would give me the help for which I yearned—how to grieve the loss of a cherished friend. As an associate pastor at an urban cathedral, and a chaplain at a major medical center, he had heard many stories of loss.

My story was one infused with anger—anger at a friend who turned a deaf ear when I expressed concern over her fatigue and weight loss. Anger over her brushing aside my suggestion to check in with a doctor. There were harsh consequences to such risky behavior. Perhaps there would have been a different outcome if she had listened. I always took her counsel seriously. Was mine not deserving of her consideration? I was angry at Anne for locking me out of this sacred and final chapter of her life. She had been there to comfort me in countless situations. Why did she not want her closest friends and even family members with her in her darkest hour, rather than throwing a blockade between her sick bed and them? She may have reaped some solace and comfort—the kind that she would have given to them in similar circumstances.

Father Bill felt the loss himself. Anne was a Daily Communicant and a volunteer at the Cathedral. After a long period of compassionate listening, he cautioned that it was not good for me to carry all of this anger inside of me. It could lead to depression. He suggested that I write Anne a letter, telling her how I felt about being shut out of her life, what her friendship meant to me, and what I would have said to her on her deathbed. He stressed the value of balance and including the good times in the letter—our love of theatre and art, the social life we enjoyed, and the spiritual bond that we shared.

"What will I do with the letter?" I asked.

"You can burn it; you can tear it up; you can bury it," was his response. I knew exactly what I would do with it. I would take it to New York and bury it there where we had spent so many happy hours together. The cloud hanging over me began to lift. I went home, pulled out my laptop and felt a surge of energy as I typed this letter.

Dear Annie,

I just returned from visiting Father Bill. He was the perfect person to whom I could pour out my grief over my loss of you. He knows both of us, and he is not afraid of women's tears. In fact, he encouraged me to shed them. So I let the dam burst and took his suggestion to write you a letter, telling you how your death has affected me. It is important that you know how devastated I am over your illness and death and what our friendship has meant.

You would have loved your funeral, burial and party afterwards. Not many have a funeral concelebrated by three priests, including Bishop Ed Conway, your boss at Catholic Charities. All of those people who had walked and danced with you through your childhood, your schools, your work life and family life were there to celebrate you. (Some had even proposed to you!) Then the funeral procession of cars following your hearse continued through Chicago's streets and into the North Shore of Chicago, where we buried you next to your parents at the family plot in Lake Forest. It is a beautiful plot under two magnificent elm trees that must have been there longer than the three generations of your Irish descendants that now call it home.

Is that really where you want to be? Wouldn't you rather be out and about with the likes of Ron and me? How is Ron going to survive without you? You had so much to live for after all of those years of working. You had a man who loved you and the resources to do what you wanted with your life.

Damn it all, Annie, why didn't you go to the doctor when I pleaded for you to go? Uterine cancer is highly curable. I had a pre-cancerous condition the year I got the divorce. The children were fourteen, sixteen and seventeen. My doctor said that if I did not have the surgery, I would probably get cancer. I even got a second opinion, for I did not want to go through that ordeal. Goodness knows I had enough on my plate with three teenagers, a demanding job and a divorce with no alimony.

After the surgery the doctor came into the recovery room to say that if I had waited six months I would have been filled with tumors. I can't imagine what the children's lives would have been like if I had postponed the surgery. Three teens without a mom seemed like history repeating itself. Going through my motherless teen years was a nightmare.

I know you were frightened of doctors. You never told me why. Were you abused by one? You were so private about your own struggles, and I didn't want to interfere with that sense of privacy. In retrospect, maybe I should have asked you.

You not only refused to take my advice, but you refused to see me. You shut everyone out of your life, except Ron. Along with Ron, your many friends and family members could have comforted you when you needed it the most. What gives? You were always there for me when I needed you.

Ron said that you couldn't bear to see all of us going on to lead healthy lives. Annie, none of us knows how much time we have. I think the real reason is that you didn't want to be vulnerable before us—writhing with pain, losing your hair, dropping pounds. Didn't you think our relationship went beyond appearances or just being there when everything is okay? Annie, I could have held your hand, wiped your brow with a cold cloth, prayed the rosary by your bedside. These gestures would have been a gift to both of us.

Now that I've vented my anger, let me share with you the treasures you brought to my life. Remember when we met in New York City? What times we had at the theatre, the old Met, dinners on the East Side, weekends in West Hampton (remember High Courage?), the Jersey Shore, and dinners at the Murphy family home in Brooklyn.

It seems that we swung between New York and Chicago like yo-yos, always looking for the right job, the right guy. Even when we were living in different cities, we'd manage to visit one another in Chicago, Florida, and Hartford, Connecticut, where I lived for 25 years, while raising my family. I wax with nostalgia as I reflect on the times you rolled out the red carpet for my kids! You took my son Tom to the English Café at Rockefeller Center, when he was only eight. He still remembers having the king salmon, while watching the skaters. The kids loved coming to your apartment overlooking Lake Michigan, pushing elevator buttons, running around the circular hallways, mesmerized by the view of Navy Pier. One of the things I celebrated when I returned to Chicago from Hartford was the fact that you were there. And now you're gone. The city will never be the same. Nor will I.

You'll be pleased that our erstwhile boyfriends, Jim and Tom, came to your wake. They were right there, grieving with the rest of us. You'll be happy to learn that Tom became a grandfather the day you were buried.

The open casket allowed me to have one last look at you. I can't believe that you had on a wig. Then I thought of you losing your hair—your crowning glory. And your hands were mere bones. You must have been down to ninety pounds. I think that I'm beginning to understand why you didn't want visitors.

Finally, Annie, thank you for just being who you were. I was so drawn to you when we first met. Your beauty, goodness, sincerity and sense of joy were not lost on me. When I was with you, I felt like I was the most important person in your life. You helped me navigate the splintered landscape of my twenties, when I was zigzagging between San Francisco, New York and Chicago. You held my hand when I was going through my divorce. And you were always front row center at the programs I gave when I launched my career counseling business in Chicago.

I yearned to be like you, and it isn't too late. You have left a legacy. As your cousin Jean said, "You left part of yourself with me." That's why I decided to leave the rose at your gravesite when everyone was handed one at the burial. Then your darling niece, Allison, gave me a petal from her rose. That went in my Bible.

Speaking of men, what a class act that Ron is! Chivalry is not dead as long as he is around. I visited him last Sunday after Mass. In the midst of his grief, he insisted on playing gentleman. When

I got up to get a glass of water, he said, "I'm the host!" Even in his pain he is thinking of others. He must have learned that from you. I felt such angst being in your physical space, encumbered with oxygen tanks, and sitting on the sofa where we used to gab for hours.

You can't believe how wonderful Katy was through all of this. She thinks I worked through some personal issues in the process—especially my mother's death. Perhaps, she added, I'll have a better understanding as to why my family handled my mother's illness the way it did. You and Ron did not want to share the truth. Neither did my family.

Thank goodness I took Father Moriarity's advice and wrote this. It is unleashing so many things that needed to get out—my anger and sadness, but also my gratitude for our friendship. I know you wouldn't want me to carry all of this anger inside of me.

I'm leaving this letter in New York, for that is where we had such memorable times. There are many choices: St. Patrick's Cathedral, the Hudson River, or burying it near the George Washington Bridge. These were all symbols of this great city that brought so much positive energy into our lives. I knew that I would discern the right place. And I did.

One day I took my granddaughter, Liana, to the Bronx Zoo. She was six. After feeding the pandas, we wandered around the adjacent park overlooking the reservoir. I had a spoon in my pocket, and Liana and I dug a small hole in the ground, near the flower beds. Then I tore up the letter in to tiny pieces and dropped it into the hole. Liana gathered the soil and covered the hole with her dainty fingers. Then we said a prayer for you. To this day I don't know what Liana said. That is between the two of you!

Stay with me, honey, and watch over Ron. I'll never forget the sight of him standing at the funeral parlor, saying, "I can't believe that this is happening." Will he ever find joy in life again? I hope that he will. I love you, Annie. Thank you for all you brought to my life and will continue to. Perhaps writing this has provided the background music in preparing for my own death.

Love, Helen

I opened my prayer book to the page where I had pressed the white rose that Allison gave me at the cemetery. Then I breathed in the autumn air, reminiscent of when Anne and I met in Manhattan. When I got home, I opened my Bible to where the dried rose petal was from Anne's burial and placed it at this verse from St. Paul's Letter to the Romans.

For if we live, we live to the Lord, and if we die, we die to the Lord. So then, whether we live or whether we die, we are the Lord's.

Romans 14:8

There is no question that Anne is with the Lord. I can't wait to join her!

REFLECTION AND JOURNALING

Lutheran Minister and Pastor Mary C. Lindberg, in her book *The Graceful Exit*, writes of a fellow pastor who went on retreat after leaving his parish of twenty years. While away he wrote letters to ten members of the congregation.

He knew he would never mail the letters, but he hoped the letters would help him release some of the emotions that churned around inside of him, an important step to his letting go.

- ❖ Have you lost someone who closed you off from his or her suffering? How did you handle it?
- ❖ Reflect on your time together and write about what that person meant to you.
- ❖ Write in your journal about how you wish he or she had shared their sufferings.
- ❖ Gather with friends and family of the deceased and share what he/she meant to you.

CHAPTER SIX

Peggy

You will always be part of me,
for you were present through so much of my unfolding.
—MACRINA WIEDERKEHR

Peggy's call came on Easter Sunday. She was phoning from her home in Wilmette. It tipped me over the edge, for my entire week had been filled with "not-so-good news." My friend Jackie had died of ovarian cancer, and Nancy, my niece and godchild, had been revisited by breast cancer. My former husband, Ed, with advanced congestive heart failure, had recently been diagnosed with Parkinson's. "So, what is your bad news?" I asked Peggy, thinking it couldn't compete with mine.

Her news bulletin was deserving of major headlines. When she and her husband, Jim, were playing in a tennis tournament in Palm Springs, she had acute abdominal distress. She cut her trip short and flew back to Chicago. "It isn't good," she repeated, as if reciting a litany.

"Peg, do you have cancer?" I blurted.

"It is pancreatic. Inoperable. It has metastasized to my liver. I have six months, if I'm lucky."

"This cannot be!" I exclaimed in disbelief.

I thought Peggy would always be there. As I glanced at the rearview mirror of our family history, I realized that she had been there for me when I was confronting health or job challenges. She had an "open door policy" for my children when they needed a place to stay during college breaks, and she was in the front row center with her friends at my daughter Katy's theatrical performances. I told her I would be there for her.

After I hung up, I darted down the hall in the Jesuit Volunteer community where I was living and shouted the "not-so-good news." There were hugs. There were prayer circles. There were admonitions: "You need to take care of yourself. Stay home from work tomorrow." "Work" was volunteer work, but I took it just as seriously as I took my high-pressure fundraising jobs in Chicago and Hartford, Connecticut. These previously homeless folks needed all the help they could get, but I would be of no use to them in this vulnerable state. The next morning I put sunglasses on my puffy eyes and walked down to St. Ignatius Chapel at Seattle University for 8:00 a.m. Mass. I lit a candle and talked to one of the Jesuits, who agreed that pancreatic cancer was one of the worst ways to go.

Even though I had only lived in Seattle for a few months, it felt like home. I came out here on a whim, when my friend Jeanette called me in Chicago to tell me that a Jesuit Volunteer ElderCorps was starting in the Northwest. "This is what you've been waiting for. You have an opportunity to live in community, adopt a simple lifestyle, deepen your spirituality, and work on behalf of the poor." I didn't have to think twice. Two months later I was in Seattle working as an advocate for the elderly poor. But now I was in a dilemma. My sister was dying, and I was far away.

Peggy dying? In addition to being my sister, she was my playmate, soul mate, and friend. I cried all night. I called my doctor and asked if there was a pill to plug up my tears; she referred me to a social worker in her clinic. She said that I didn't need a pill; I just needed to keep on crying. I went to Swedish Hospital in my neighborhood and enrolled in a support group for families of those with cancer. I talked to Father Ryan, the pastor of St. James Cathedral. His father died of pancreatic cancer when he was in his fifties. "I was in the seminary in Rome. He was gone within a few months," he said. "It is a horrible disease." Sensing the urgency, I made my reservations to fly to Chicago.

The next week I was strolling with Peggy along the Lake Michigan beach in front of the house where we grew up. With the lake breezes at our backs, we waxed nostalgic as we walked along the beach where long ago we swam, sunbathed, and flirted with the lifeguards. Now, during our strolls we hugged, we cried, we laughed, and we were silent. We paused in front of the family home, which we had left fifty years earlier, and reminisced about the sweet times that had been lost and that could never be recaptured. This is where some of the best parties on Chicago's North Shore took place. It is where, at fourteen, I caught my sister Marie's bouquet at her wedding reception. It is where Stan gave me my first "real kiss" on our front porch, before he went off to the Korean War. And it is where my mother died after ten years of fighting a losing battle with Parkinson's.

The heaviness in our hearts weighed on us like the anchors of the boats moored by the beach. Peggy said, "I made a deal with God. He can have me, but there are three things I want to happen first: Attend my grandson Henry's First Communion and my granddaughter Meggie's high school graduation, and see my daughter Barbara's adopted Chinese baby girl." That was so like Peggy—articulate and focused. Her requests seemed reasonable to me.

My sister Marie and my brother, Jim, and I worked out a schedule so one of us would be with Peggy most of the time. In the meantime, Peggy was embraced by her eight children, fifteen grandchildren, and a plethora of friends. Neighbors took turns driving her to the University of Chicago Hospital for chemotherapy; her refrigerator overflowed with enough healthy food to feed her and her visitors. And there were the prayer sessions, which fed her spirit and those of us who were digesting the shock of her grim diagnosis. Every Thursday morning members of Peggy's growing support system were in her living room. They read Scripture, recited the rosary, and did reflections. Katy sang the 23rd Psalm.

The Lord is my shepherd; I shall not want.
He maketh me to lie down in green pastures: he leadeth me beside the still waters.
He restoreth my soul: he leadeth me in the paths of righteousness for his name's sake.
Yea, though I walk through the valley of the shadow of death, I will fear no evil: for thou art with me; thy rod and thy staff they comfort me.
Thou preparest a table before me in the presence of mine enemies; thou anointest my head with oil; my cup runneth over.
Surely goodness and mercy shall follow me all of the days of my life: and I will dwell in the house of the Lord forever.

When I took Peggy to Chicago for her treatment, one would think she was going to the symphony. She would leave the house always looking her best and wearing fashionable outfits. What a deceiving ensemble considering how ill she was. As we drove along Chicago's Outer Drive, we talked about suffering. "I have tried to live a good life. Why is this happening to me?" I did not have an answer. Philosophers and theologians have explored the question of suffering since the beginning of time.

I told her that if we believe that Christ suffered so we could go to heaven, then we know that she was going to be up there, healed of this wretched disease and rewarded for all that she had done for the family she raised, the homeless women she fed, the children she taught to write exciting prose and poetry, the neighbors she comforted, and the ways she served the Church.

One morning, when Peggy was struggling with the chemo side effects, I poured us a cup of tea, arranged extra pillows on her sofa, and put a quilt over her weary body. I sat down next to her, put my arm around her slumped shoulders, and read St. Paul's Epistle to the Romans 8:24.

> *For in hope we have been saved, but hope that is seen is not hope; for who hopes for what he already sees? But if we hope for what we do not see, with perseverance we wait eagerly for it.*

This passage was intended for the likes of us, for there was not much hope on that sofa. There was no logical reason to be optimistic. All of her lab results pointed to the fact that Peggy was dying. The chemo was a last-ditch effort to reverse those odds, but we weren't fooling ourselves. Once those cancer cells attack the liver, it is a death knell. Nevertheless, despite all those predictions, St. Paul would have still held out hope. So why can't we? Peggy sat there, taking it in, as the two of us pondered this message.

I treasured the time we had together. How best to spend it? Perhaps interject some lightness and beauty in Peggy's day? Glancing at her blank dining room wall, I asked, "Peg, you have that wonderful collection of English teacups, and it is just gathering dust in your sideboard drawer. What would you think of displaying those cups on a mahogany shelf on that wall? I'll go over to the antique mall while you take your nap." Dazed, she nodded approval.

As I meandered through the mall, I spotted a sign, "English Antique Emporium." I saw a large bowl with the same vibrant greens, oranges and turquoises of Peggy's living room and the delicacy that only fine porcelain can resemble. It was the last thing Peggy would have bought for herself. After all, in a household of eight children, one does not engage in frivolities. It is simply a challenge to prepare the meals and get them on the table!

Now the children had their own homes, and Peggy's days were numbered. She had earned some frivolity. "I'll take it," I told the saleswoman. Thoughts of a mahogany teacup shelf evaporated when I handed over my Visa. I would have to dip into my savings to pay for this treasure. No big deal. I had done that for things that were important to me—paying the children's private school tuition, making a gift to a homeless shelter, or reimbursing my landlord for reducing my rent when I lost my job. My sister of 58 years was at death's door. She had been divested of so much that defined her. How many more opportunities would I have to add some grace to her life?

Peggy was napping when I returned from my shopping adventure. I gingerly placed the bowl on the dining room table. My instincts were right. The colors highlighted those of the living room upholstery and artwork, and even the pedestal blended in with the table. It was a marriage that was meant to be! As Peggy struggled down the hallway, robe draped around her stooped shoulders and clutching the heating pad to her abdomen, I steered her into the dining room. She just stood there in silence. Finally, she spoke.

"What is this? Where did it come from? I don't understand."

"Peggy, I hope you don't mind. Instead of the teacup shelf, I bought this. Somehow it just seemed to have your name on it."

We sat down and had a cup of tea at the dining room table. Peggy's eyes were glued to the bowl. Her awed silence was her thank you. This was a perfect note on which to depart, for I had to leave for Seattle the next day.

One of the things that kept me afloat between trips to Chicago was the support I received from the Seattle community. My Jesuit Volunteer community offered prayers for Peggy every night. One of the homeless clients I served wrote a prayer for her. Father Ryan was continually asking about Peggy, and Sister Anne, pastoral associate at St. James, told me that she wanted me to call her when Peggy died. My fellow Cabrini Ministers–

those who were involved in ministering to the sick and vulnerable–offered prayers for Peggy. And the social worker and cancer support group at Swedish Hospital provided a safe place for me to weep. This all gave me an emotional ballast for my upcoming trip to Chicago, which I suspected might be my last, given the news I received from the family concerning Peggy's health status. This time my visit to her would not be at her home, but in a Hospice unit, where I went immediately upon my arrival in Wilmette.

Peggy remained there for a week, with her children taking turns spending the night in her room. One night her daughter Barbara arrived with her backpack, made up her cot, tucked in her mom, and gave her a big smack on the check. "I love you, Mom." Then she checked in with the nurse on duty, who had been in close touch with the doctor. She and the doctor went into the family consultation room.

The doctor told Barbara that she had exhausted every form of treatment. The disease was irreversible. When the doctor came in with Barbara the next day to tell Peggy that it was time for her to go home to die, Peggy's circle of friends surrounded her. They were the moms whose children were classmates of her youngest child, Margie. They were there for each other, good times and bad. It's hard to tell which this was, for there was nothing but goodness and love in that room. I kissed Peggy good-bye before I left for the airport to return to Seattle. While fighting back the fountain of tears about to burst inside of me, I wondered if I'd see her again.

Peggy's friends reached out to her by reaching out to me. They took turns making their homes available to me, so that I wouldn't have to stay at a hotel. They transported me to the airport. They prayed with me. Mary was one of them. She was well acquainted with cancer, having lost a teenage son to bone cancer. Mary lived just a few blocks from Peggy and put my name on her guest room. She drove me to O'Hare Airport for my flight back to Seattle. While on the plane, I had intense abdominal pain, and my abdomen was swollen. Are these sympathy pains for Peggy? I told the stewardess, who paged a doctor. There was one across the aisle from me, clad in jeans and a plaid shirt. She felt my abdomen and gave me news I didn't want to hear.

"You have an abdominal obstruction. This is serious. You need to go to an emergency room immediately. I'll tell the pilot to make an emergency landing."

We were two hours away from Seattle, somewhere around Utah, and I was not about to inconvenience over 300 passengers. "I'll take a chance and wait," was my response.

The ambulance waited at the gate; the driver put on the siren and sped down I-5 to the University of Washington Medical Center. I *did* have an obstruction and was admitted, with a gastric nasal tube down my esophagus. My brother, Jim, called to tell me that Peggy was in a coma. The tube didn't prevent the tears from flowing. I told the doctors that I had to be in Wilmette for my sister's death. They said that my situation was serious; that I might need abdominal surgery to remove the blockage. What if I died, too? Two funerals in a week! One in Wilmette, another in Seattle! My poor family.

St. James arranged to have a Cabrini Volunteer call me every few hours and pray with me. Her name was Ann, and her comforting voice immediately calmed me. She is now one of my most trusted, loyal friends who continues to minister to me during my physical and spiritual challenges.

I recovered and made it back to Chicago to find Peggy still in a coma. She was in a hospital bed in the guest room at home. The family was standing watch with the Hospice team. There were candles. There were chants. There were massages. There was Mozart. There was a tank of oxygen. I gave her morphine drops. I held her hand. I prayed the rosary.

I was at her bedside when she took her last breath. So was her husband, Jim, her daughter Margie, our sister Marie and her husband, Vin, and my son Ed. With that last breath all the tension in Peggy's body escaped, and her face was transformed into that of an angel. She had the most radiant smile I'd ever seen. She was home in heaven. All the pain was behind her. I called Sister Anne at St. James to tell her that Peggy was gone.

There was much to do in preparation for Peggy's wake and funeral. Assignments were given out by Barbara—the investment banker. Mine was to write Peggy's obituary. Just two years before, I had done her resume, for she was exploring a job opportunity with an educational publishing firm. Peggy had done so much, and I wanted to be sure that her volunteer and professional work were recognized.

"She could motivate her students to write in the most creative ways, using story-telling as a tool," said the principal of St. Vincent's–a Chicago inner-city school where Peggy taught English. It saddens me that Peggy never wrote her life story, an irony since she spent 25 years teaching kids how to write theirs. Why didn't she write her own? One day she told me that she didn't think that she had done much with her life. Not done much with her life?

There were 700 people at her wake–the largest in Donnellan Funeral Home's 90-year history. Each of these 700 had their own story to tell of the ways she loved them. The extended family represented about 100 of those. But there were many we didn't know: her students, homeless women, clerks at the Jewel Grocers, those who heard her read Scripture at St. Athanasius Church, the children at her grandson Henry's school, and her seventh graders. One of her student's mothers said that her bashful, awkward sixth-grader blossomed under Peggy's tutelage, when he played the lead in "Peter Pan." A former student who gave a eulogy said that thanks to Peggy he would never spell development with an "e" after the "p."

She was smiling down on all of us, pain-free at last. It was time to say good-bye to her family and to my children. When would I be back? Would Peggy and Jim's house still be here? I could not imagine walking into that place without Peggy in it. But now it was time to focus on my Seattle life.

Upon returning to Seattle I went to St. James to have a Mass said for Peggy. Father Ryan and Sister Anne embraced me as they offered their sympathy. "Oh, to lose a sister," said Father Ryan. "I will offer my Mass today for her," and he announced it to the assembly. The next Sunday, Mia Vera, a parishioner whom I barely knew, handed me a book on grief. "This place wasn't the same without you," she said. What a welcome home!

Several weeks later, I returned to Peggy's home to help the family prepare to put the house on the market. It was a shock to walk into the room where she died and see a new bed, a clean carpet, and no oxygen tank. All the medicine bottles, prayers, and holy cards were off the dresser. Her closet was empty. It seems that she was divested of so much that defined her.

That night I wrote a journal entry, reflecting on all that had happened these past few days. I reflected: "Peggy, there is less and less of you here now. What is it like in heaven? One thing is for sure—I know you are at peace. It was written all over your face when you left this world and went to the next. I hope that you are so content in your new life that you're no longer mad at God. Are you really just a spirit until your body is united with your soul after the Second Coming? I can't imagine you being a spirit, for you are so physical and passionate. Do you see much of Mother and Daddy, Kathy McNulty and the zillions of friends you have up there? Perhaps death was your liberator. I hope so."

Before leaving, I strolled along the Evanston lake front before I boarded the plane for Seattle. Autumn was Peggy's favorite time for walking on the beach. She loved the colors and the quiet. Reflecting on last spring's stroll, with both of us carrying knots in our hearts over that grim diagnosis, the knots began to unravel.

"You know, God didn't go along with your plan, Peggy. I guess He couldn't wait for Henry's First Communion, Meggie's high school graduation or the arrival of your Chinese granddaughter. But is it a coincidence that Meggie's graduation turned out to be on your birthday?"

I was increasingly aware that there never is a "perfect" time to die, for time is not a friend to death and grief.

REFLECTION AND JOURNALING

In our sleep, pain that cannot forget falls drop by drop upon the heart and in our despair, against our will, comes wisdom from the awful grace of God.

—Aeschylus

- Reflect on some of the life-giving steps I took during Peggy's illness.
- Have you ever received news from a loved one of a serious diagnosis? What was your response? What did you learn from that experience?
- Did someone guide you through this time? Was that a friend, family member, your faith community, or a counselor? Which of them was most helpful?
- What do you suggest for those who are searching for ways to cope with their grief?

CHAPTER SEVEN

Ed

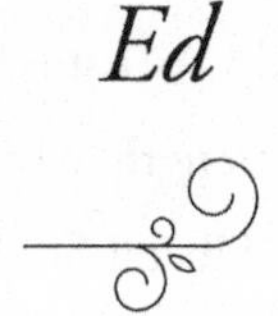

I found the process transformative. I was convinced I wouldn't survive it, but I did. I was grateful for grief.

—Kate Goehring

It was Christmas Eve. I had flown from Seattle, Washington, to St. Petersburg, Florida, to say goodbye to my former husband, Ed, who was dying. I was dreading facing Ed's exit from this world and all that it involved—suffering, tears, and regrets of things said or not said. My trepidation was lessened only by the prospect of seeing our children, now 40, 42, and 43. I passed the crèche in the lobby of St. Anthony's Hospital, with the Holy Family tucked inside, and thought of *my* family and the vulnerability it was sharing with *this* Family that changed history. Vulnerability is a word I never applied to Ed. He was a robust and an "I'm in charge" kind of fellow, so I did not recognize the fragile figure when I walked into Cubicle 55 in the Intensive Care Unit. This was in stark contrast to the man with whom we'd celebrated Thanksgiving just a month before. He was still well enough to be attending philosophy classes at Eckard College—a program for retirees. The man in the ICU was dependent on a machine for his every breath. Ed was about to get a call from God, but he was on hold. What could be more vulnerable than that?

Our children had flown in the night before, when Ed had emergency surgery for a perforated colon. The doctor doubted that he would survive the surgery, but he did, just barely. As I surveyed the cubicle, I marveled at our children and their steadfast strength. My eldest, Ed Jr., was professor of music history in the Program of Liberal Studies at the University of Notre Dame. Then there was Tom, a jazz musician and composer in New York, and the youngest, Katy, was an actor in New York. All of us were independent and successful, yet in this moment we were all helpless pilgrims on a rocky shore. My feelings in St. Petersburg, where folks romped in the warm surf, were of gratitude for what our children and I were able to bring to Ed's bedside.

In Cubicle 55 we were decked out in sterile, crinkled yellow paper gowns with matching rubber gloves, masks, and hats. We donned them like royal robes, for we couldn't risk adding to Ed's illness by giving him our germs. Because we didn't know if he'd make it through the night, we decided to forego our tradition of opening gifts on Christmas and did so on Christmas Eve. Between the ventilator and IVs, Ed couldn't tackle the presents. Tom, our middle child, peeled off the bright red foil with silver bells and proudly displayed the Pittsburgh Steelers sweatshirt, as if he were presenting his father with the Olympic Gold Medal. Ed would never wear this shirt with a symbol of his hometown's football team, but it is was a good move on Tom's part, and we were an attentive audience. Katy gave him a photo from her role in "Angels in America," the Tony Kushner play in which she was cast as Harper on the national tour for which he'd proudly considered himself her "Stage Door Johnnie." Ed Jr. presented his father and me with bright red and green packages with red satin ribbons perched on top. Inside were copies of his newly published book, *Three Modes of Perception in Mozart—The Philosophical, the Pastoral, and Comic in* Così Fan Tutte. I opened the cover and saw that he had dedicated it to us. My copy bears this inscription:

Dear M,

Here you are a co-dedicatee of My Book . . . I remember many times when I was wondering if music history was the right field for me or whether I would do well. And I remember your being there to help me through those times. Most of all, I think it was from you that I learned to follow what I love.

Love, E

Back in Cubicle 55, we planned to give Ed the best gift of all—the opportunity to breathe on his own. If he remained on the ventilator much longer, he would not shake this infection. But we had no idea what would happen when the nurse removed the machine. Ed, Tom, Katy, and I went into the hall and huddled in a circle like the Notre Dame offense negotiating its next play. We held hands, said the "Our Father," and elected Ed Jr. the quarterback to negotiate the removal of this machine with the doctor. The nurse arranged for us to be on speakerphone.

"What are the odds that my father will die when he is removed from life support?" asked Ed.

"The odds are about sixty percent that he will be able to breathe on his own," replied the doctor.

Ed responded, "I want to be sure that my father has the most comfort available to him. What are the risks involved? Will it hurt when the ventilator is removed? Will he be able to eat or drink afterwards?"

What a stellar man young Ed is. Always at the head of his class, tonight he graduated *summa cum laude* in compassion. I am in awe of all three of our children as they gather information on how to best care for their father. They are, indeed, displaying gifts their father and I fostered: getting at the truth, understanding possible outcomes, and taking responsibility for those choices. But mostly it was the tenderness with which they embraced their father that touched me so.

Tom kissed him on the forehead. "I love you, Dad."

Ed Jr. squeezed his arm and kissed him on the check. "Hang in there, Dad."

Katy put her head on his chest: "Dadden."

I took his boney hand, kissed him on the forehead, and said, "I love you, Ed."

There was a time when I said, "I love you, Ed," and I wasn't sure that I meant it. It was the first time he kissed me. We were parked in front of my father's apartment after seeing *King Lear*. Ed's wife, Betty, had died of ovarian cancer the year before, at age 38. He was still grieving when we met at the baptism of my sister Peggy's sixth child. Peggy and her husband, Jim, were friends of Betty and Ed's, and they felt that Ed and I would have a lot in common. "He is quite intellectual and loves the arts. I think you'll enjoy each other," Peggy said. So, when this attractive "mature" man came up to me at the reception after the baptism, hand extended, saying, "You must be Helen," I felt a connection.

The next Saturday we went to the Impressionists exhibit at the Art Institute of Chicago; the following Saturday we took in Byron Janis's interpretation of Mozart's 21st Piano Concerto at the Chicago Symphony. Afterwards we went to dinner at The Rib, on Chicago's North Side, where we discussed Teilhard de Chardin, the Jesuit paleontologist. Then we started attending Mass at Holy Name Cathedral. He was forty; I was twenty-eight. When Ed told me one night in the car that he loved me, I didn't say anything. The next time he kissed me, he asked me if I loved him, and I said "yes." How do people know when they're in love? If I said, "No, I don't love you," he would be hurt, and I didn't want to do that after all he had been through. As I look through the rearview mirror of my life, I think my desire to please trumped the value of honesty.

As my mind raced through memories of years ago, back in Cubicle 55 there was a stillness that echoed as the nurse cautiously lifted the ventilator, allowing Ed to breath. We circled his bed and held our breath as Ed teetered on the edge of life. He took his first independent breath in three days! We all emitted a sigh of relief, and the nurse suggested that we leave, for Ed had been through a lot those last few hours. The children and I went back to Ed's condo. I checked my email, not expecting anyone to send one on Christmas, but there was "Ann" appearing in my "Inbox." I had met Ann at St. James Cathedral. Being in her presence was being on Holy Ground. She taught me how to listen. She taught me about Centering Prayer. She taught me how to be a friend by being one, even on Christmas.

Dear Helen,

Your children have so lovingly responded to their father's decline. Blessings for peaceful moments together and potentially, a final good-bye.

Love, Ann

We had already received the gift of peaceful moments together.

The next day Ed Sr. graduated from the ICU to Room 106 of the medical floor. His life was still on hold. So were our jobs and relationships. Katy was in rehearsal for *Law and Order.* Tom's vacation time at the New York investment banking firm where he worked in between jazz gigs was used up. Ed was due back in South Bend to administer final exams to his music history class. I was overseeing an endowment campaign at Seattle's Horizon House, the retirement home where I was Director of Philanthropy. The doctors said that Ed could go at any time, or he could live a year. I couldn't imagine leaving him now. We wouldn't forgive ourselves if he died alone.

"I'll stay for another week," I blurted.

Our children were stunned that I would choose to spend my precious vacation days at St. Anthony's Hospital. I had divorced their father. I had no obligation to be there. But it simply seemed the right thing to do, as divorcing him was also the right thing, although the most painful choice I ever made. I left Ed thirty years ago because I could not live with him anymore. Job losses, depression, and differences on how to spend money and time created a landscape replete with boulders and pitfalls. There were times when silence reigned supreme, but those silences did not suppress the anger seething beneath the unsettling terrain. Raising three adolescents in this fractious household would not be a healthy model for a harmonious marriage. I left him when the children were fourteen, sixteen, and seventeen. Why couldn't I leave him now?

No one should die alone, and certainly not a man with whom I shared eighteen years and three children. I thought of my mother and the vigil our family held around her bed some 57 years ago. I did not afford myself "the luxury" to mourn the most important person in my life—my dear mother who loved me unconditionally, despite her frailty and vulnerability. Maybe this was an opportunity to bring my own life back to healing during the thin slice remaining to me. So, on the day after Christmas, I wondered how I would spend my time with this man who I hadn't lived with for thirty years. "I'll figure that out when I get back to his apartment," I mused.

When I entered Ed's apartment, I spotted Mary Oliver's *Why I Wake Early* on the coffee table. I was so glad I tossed this anthology of poetry into my suitcase. My friend Mary, a resident of Horizon House, gave it to me. Oliver's poems were like prayers and seemed to be written just for me. I tucked the book in my backpack for my next day's visit with Ed.

"Ed, I have Mary Oliver's poetry here. Would you like me to read some of her poems?" He nods. I read several of these gems and ask if he wants me to continue. Another nod. "Is there any special one that you like?" I read the titles again, and he does a double nod when I mention *Why I Wake Early*, the book's title.

> Hello, sun in my face.
> Hello, you who make the morning
> And spread it over the fields and into
> the faces of the tulips and the nodding
> morning glories, and into the windows
> of, even, the miserable and the crotchety.

If anyone has reason to be miserable and crotchety, Ed does. For a man who loves to be in control, he is not. He can't control his bladder; he can't control his bowels; he can't talk or swallow. Maybe that is what death is about—losing all that you value so you have no baggage to take to heaven. I think of my Jesuit friend Father Pat O'Brien's homily on St. Matthew's Gospel, in which Christ refers to entering heaven by the narrow gate. Father says the narrow gate is vulnerability, getting old, being out of control, having your body surprise you every day. "People in this unit are all on their way out," says Sharon, the head nurse on ICU. "They reflect on their lives, the things they wish they had done differently, and how to use the time left."

Ed doesn't waste a second. There are lots of angels helping in this transition. One angel in Florida is Joan Dunne, who insists that I stay at her waterfront home in St. Pete's Beach, which is the community where Ed lived. Joan's ministry of hospitality is a balm to my weary body and spirit. After doing the drill at St. Anthony's, I perch myself on her dock, like a seagull. Merlot in hand, I wrap my arms around the sunset and just *be*.

How grateful I am for the apologies of two years ago, when I shared my regrets for not showing my appreciation for his helping me with the children when I was in graduate school, and they were all toddlers. He extended an olive branch for the blasts of anger that he hurled my way during the divorce and the silences that sucked the oxygen out of the air. These confessions did more than wipe the stains of unkindness from our souls. I never experienced such intimacy in our marriage as I did in that hospital. There wasn't time for such closeness as we cared for our three children in diapers, one of whom had milk allergies and colic. We were completely consumed with raising a family but not with nurturing our marriage. We nursed our kids through the measles, chicken pox, and mumps, helped them with homework, cheered them on at Little League games, attended recitals, and wouldn't think of missing a teacher's conference.

Amidst these activities, our lives took unforeseen turns: job losses and moves, new schools, new neighborhoods, illnesses. Sadness seemed to be seeping into our rooms. Sadness over our budget; sadness over how we spent our time; sadness over his put-downs. Ours was a lonely marriage. We didn't have many friends. I think part of it was our age difference; but our life outlook was also at odds. His Teutonic (German) and my Celtic (Irish) temperaments were not a good recipe for harmony. I always felt that there would be better times ahead; Ed was convinced that disaster lurked in our hallways.

The hospital corridors became familiar territory as I walked them daily to visit Ed. They began to represent our journey of healing: his was toward death; mine was into grief, as I stood watch by his bedside. Witnessing Ed's final days conjured up memories of my mother's passing, and I found myself grieving her once again. Unlike my childhood grief, my grief for Ed was witnessed by a supportive community of family and friends.

As I walked the circuitous path of Ed's last days, I was given a hand up by folks on the other coast. Father Mike Ryan, the pastor of St. James Cathedral, said, "Helen, you are bearing witness, and no one can take that grace from you." My spiritual director, Terri, also found meaning in these events. "You have come to a deep place, being able to speak for Ed and express your feelings. This is a time of reconciliation," she said when I called her in Seattle from St. Pete's Beach. Tonight, I had a message from Peg, a dear friend and soul mate—a safe haven in this storm. Although in Hawaii on vacation, she was walking this path with me on the other side of the globe. I named her emails "cyberspace prayers" traversing from the Pacific to the Atlantic Ocean.

Dear Helen,

I am glad that your heart is at peace, and that you're proving reconciliation with Ed. You're modeling something valuable to your circle. Maybe Ed just needs to hang on to experience every bit of that, who knows?

Nite, nite.

Peg

So in between Mary Oliver, Peg's emails, and the *Magnificat*—a prayer book that Ed and I both read daily—it seemed that we had put the harsh headwinds of divorce behind us.

"Mrs. Goehring, we've been trying to reach you," the head nurse says with a sense of urgency as I pass the nurse's station the next morning.

"Your husband has gone into V-Tach—a serious heart arrhythmia." I sprint down the corridor to Room 106. The heart monitor displays the EKG lines zigzagging on its capricious path. The nurse directs me to the patient lounge for a conference call with the children. That means pulling Katy out of rehearsal, Tom away from his office and Ed Jr. out of class.

"Are we going to move Ed from Level A, to *resuscitate*, or to Level B, which includes *DNR, plus comfort care only*?" That was the ultimate question posed by the head nurse. Since I was no longer married to Ed, I didn't have a say in these end-of-life issues. I think of Joan Didion's book *The Year of Magical Thinking,* in which, after witnessing her husband's death, she says that "death needs to be embraced, not stage-managed. Death is illusive, unpredictable and tricky—it is easier if one just embraces it." I b r e a t h e.

I tell the children that I must return to Seattle, for I have work responsibilities. Tom arranges to replace me as his father's watchman. I take Ed's boney hand and pray the rosary with the beads I bought him at St. James Cathedral and had blessed by Father Ryan. I tell him that I'm returning to Seattle, and that Tom will come the next day. I read the *Magnificat*—the Song of Mary taken from the Gospel of Luke. This canticle was spoken by the Virgin Mary at her Visitation to her cousin, Elizabeth, and is often sung in Catholic churches as part of evening liturgy. It is one of Ed's favorite prayers. I kiss him on the forehead; thanking him for the good times, helping me with my term papers in grad school and most of all, raising three decent and accomplished children. I depart with a heavy heart, knowing that the next time I see him, he will be in a casket. Reflecting back on the night Ed asked me if I loved him, I wasn't sure then. But I am now. I thought of St. Augustine's words from his *Confessions*, "Late Have I Loved You":

> Late have I loved you, beauty so old and so new: late have I loved you. And see, you were within and I was in the external world and sought you there, and in my unlovely state I plunged into those lovely created things which you made. You were with me, and I was not with you. The lovely things kept me far from you, though if they did not have their existence in you, they had no existence at all. You called and cried out loud and shattered my deafness. . . . I tasted you, and I feel but hunger and thirst for you. You touched me, and I am set on fire to attain the peace which is yours.

On the plane back to Seattle, I reflected on those final weeks with Ed. I felt a sense of peace. Ed's last days were a gift to all of us. Even though we were all involved in an awkward dance, we were in step with one another for the first time in years. Gathering around his bedside in the ICU, exchanging presents, reading Mary Oliver, holding his hand, and all of us telling him how much he was loved. "Mom, we're doing it the right way," said Katy.

Katy replaced Tom as Ed's caretaker after he spent a week with his father. She had been with Ed every day, reading to him, praying with him, and discussing his treatment and care with the doctors. On the day before Valentine's Day, she asked him: "Will you be my Valentine tomorrow, Dad?" Unable to speak, he nodded. "Can I be yours?" he nodded to that, too. She'd planned to present him with a bouquet of red roses the next day. But dozing off to sleep that night, she received a call from the nurse's station. "I think you should come back and hold your father's hand." She had not packed black for this trip. How could this be? Again, the response was: "I think you should come back and hold your father's hand." Katy threw her coat over her pajamas (her father's frayed Sedona T-Shirt and some boxer shorts) and drove frantically to the hospital. She missed his last breath but got the first few moments after that; his body was still warm.

The nurse told Katy that she could stay with him until the team arrived to take him to the morgue. His body was free of the ever-present and debilitating Parkinson's disease for the first time in many years. He was free of congestive heart failure. Free of bladder cancer. Free of the black cloud of depression that hovered over our marriage. Katy sat on the edge of the bed, holding him in her arms, just as he used to hold her when rocking her to sleep as a toddler. She pulled the volume of *Yeats' Collected Works* he'd kept on his shelf (and read) since she'd given it to him her freshman year of college, the inside inscription reading, "Dad, here's to your journey and mine." She read a poem he'd all but memorized:

The Cloths of Heaven

Had I the heaven's embroidered cloths,
Enwrought with golden and silver light,
The blue and the dim and the dark cloths
Of night and light and the half-light;

I would spread the cloths under your feet:
But I, being poor, have only my dreams;
I have spread my dreams under your feet;
Tread softly because you tread on my dreams.

"I was grateful to be alone with him in the hours after he passed away. I was grateful that they let me hold him. And I was grateful that for some reason we'd packed his Yeats when he'd entered the ICU. 'Tread softly, for you tread on my dreams. . . .'" She said that she was anything but happy. "But boy was I aware of the closeness of God!"

I flew to St. Pete's the next day and stayed at Ed's apartment. While the children made the funeral arrangements, met with his financial advisor, and closed his bank accounts, they asked me to sort through their father's possessions. Exploring his library was a journey of discovery, ranging from Mortimer Adler to John Paul II to Tolstoy. If I found these books in another library, my response would be, "I want to meet this person. What a breadth of knowledge!"

The children and I were assembled in the oak-paneled parlor of Brett Funeral Home in St. Petersburg. They did not have to include me in this meeting, so I acted as a silent observer, except when asked to weigh in on a matter where my participation could simplify the planning; there were so many decisions to be made. What kind of funeral do you want? Have you selected pallbearers? Who will give the eulogy?

Our children—now just "my" children—had all the right instincts. "Traditional, Catholic, military, simple," they all chimed in.

At this final adieu to Ed, I felt a sense of gratitude and wonder that the children managed to follow their bliss, choosing careers and lives suited to their passions and aptitudes. How different Ed's life might have been if he had pursued a less rocky path without such bleak boundaries and often without harmony. Ed and I were like two lost souls, largely unable to help each other or ourselves. But we were able to find peace together, there in St. Andrew's Hospital, with our beloved children there with us. I thought back to Christmas Eve, when the children and I had put on those sterile masks before entering the ICU to comfort Ed and each other as he faced death. Although I wore an actual physical mask in the ICU, I was never so "unmasked." The masks I had been wearing—pretending that things were okay, when our marriage was unraveling—had fallen away. It is surprising how much better the world looks when one takes off her mask!

Tread softly, for you tread on my dreams.

—William Butler Yeats

REFLECTION AND JOURNALING

This was a death that brought healing to everyone involved. It brought healing to us as a family, for all of us were united around Ed's death bed, saying our final good-byes. It brought healing to me, for I was able to erase the trauma of divorce and remember the blessings in our marriage. And it brought healing to my husband as he was able to depart from this world knowing that he was forgiven, loved, and cared for.

- Describe the experience of the death of someone close to you who you found it hard to forgive. Name ways it impacted your life.
- What did others do to comfort you?
- Write about the ways you comforted yourself.
- If you had a friend whose divorced spouse was close to death, how would you counsel him or her to spend those last moments?

CHAPTER EIGHT

Steve

"Grief changes you. You do not need to leave your grief b›ind in order to live a newly beautiful life."

—Megan Devine

Helen, do you have a minute?" queried my fellow parishioner Steve. I was leaving 5:30 Mass at St. James Cathedral in Seattle and was on my way home. What a gentleman, I thought, as he held the cathedral door for me. Steve was one of the few men I knew who still held doors for women and wore a shirt and tie. He was wearing a blue and gray-striped tie with a blue V-necked sweater and a starched white shirt. Even without these trappings, he was handsome. I wondered what Steve had on his mind tonight, for he appeared anxious.

"Helen, I've not been feeling well. After a battery of tests, I've learned that I have pancreatic cancer. The doctor said that I have two to nine months to live."

"Oh my God," I whispered to myself. We stood at the bus stop, our raincoats like blotters soaking in the Seattle drizzle. I dove into an ocean of thoughts and surfaced with no answers. Steve opened a briefcase with medicine bottles lined up as if they are soldiers marching off to war. His weapons included pills for pain, indigestion, and Lord knows what else. There we were standing on the corner of Marion St. and Terry Ave., heavy hearts joined.

Three months earlier, a community clinic had dismissed Steve's persistent abdominal distress as acid reflux and gave him a bottle of antacids. The disease festered until one night he was rushed to the hospital, writhing with abdominal pain. Tests revealed a tumor on his pancreas. Why hadn't the clinic done an ultrasound? Perhaps the cancer could have been arrested if caught in the early stages.

Steve turned on the faucet of his anxieties, and I listened. "I don't know where to begin. What do I do with my possessions? Will I have enough money to pay for my care? How do I want to spend my last days? Where will I die—at home, in the hospital? Nothing has prepared me for this! I'm so alone."

"What about your family? Are any of them nearby?"

"They are in Cleveland, and I rarely see them. My real community is in Seattle."

"Steve, there are so many who care about you at St. James. You won't be alone. I could have a gathering of your friends at my place, where we can pray and show our support for you."

I told him about my sister Peggy, who had died of pancreatic cancer. When she was diagnosed, family and friends assembled at her home outside of Chicago. We prayed the rosary; my daughter, Katy, sang the 23rd Psalm. Others read Mary Oliver's poetry or sat silently by Peggy, as she looked death in the face. He said he'd think about my offer to have a similar gathering.

The next morning I told a Hospice worker about Steve. That afternoon she left Steve his first voicemail since his diagnosis. I made four calls on my lunch hour. In response, Lisa brought a bowl of soup; Joyce stopped by with a rosary; Eryn called him; Kathy brought flowers from her garden. At the next St James ministry meeting, others unknown to him offered help. John could stop by to pray the rosary; Stuart would visit weekly. Pat, who is grieving her son's suicide, could invite him to join her on a walk through the Arboretum.

When I told Steve of these gestures, he blurted, "Why would people do this? They don't know me." I couldn't answer that question. But there was something about Steve and his situation that touched people at their core. Perhaps they envisioned themselves in similar circumstances.

So, who was this Steve with whom I was spending his last days on earth? He was a complex man with innumerable talents. I discovered this at our first Rite of Christian Initiation for Adults (RCIA) session. The RCIA prepares people for entering the Catholic Church. Steve and I were learning to be sponsors for these candidates and were required to attend meetings one evening a week for eight months. It was a rigorous program, but Steve's presence made the time go faster. His responses to presentations on the sacraments, grace and Scripture were insightful and enlightening. Given his background, that was no surprise.

Stricken with polio at the age of two, during childhood he was unable to participate in the sports activities of most "normal" Midwestern boys. There were no baseball bats, footballs, or ice skates in Steve's closet. Instead, on his bedroom bookshelf there were the *Encyclopedia Britannica*, the Bible, Latin grammar books, and volumes of H. G. Wells and Toynbee. In his modest home in West Seattle one would find Dante, the *New York Times*, and *Lives of the Saints.*

A few weeks before Steve started chemotherapy, he was off to Ars, France, where St. Jean-Baptiste-Marie Vianney (the Curé of Ars) spent his days praying on behalf of the poor, the sick, and penitents.

Steve opined, "This is something I must do. My mortality is staring me in my face. Maybe I'll find some answers and the grace to get through this. If this is what God wants of me, I'll accept it."

But Ars did not have the comfort and security that such a vulnerable pilgrim required. The hard mattress and damp quarters of the 300-year-old monastery were a burden. Worst of all, Steve couldn't reach his doctor to increase the dosage of his pain medication. He yearned for the comforts of home and his health care team. And he knew that the sooner he started on the chemo, the better the prospects of zapping those tumors. He left Ars two weeks before his scheduled departure and began his first round of chemotherapy. This assault on his system was more intense than he anticipated. When he would call me, his voice was a mere whisper.

"Helen, I am staring my mortality in the face. If God wants me, I pray that I will be ready to go. But it's so frightening. How should I spend my final days? I want each hour to count."

Clinging to the only plank he had left in the river of life, he was facing death, and he was frightened. But he didn't let that fear—whether of pain, dying alone, or saying his good-byes—rob him of a moment's living. How could I help him live the life he wanted to live and make each hour count? First, I made sure that he was visited and supported by the clergy.

Father Ryan, the pastor of St. James Cathedral, called Steve every two weeks; and a Catholic deacon visited Steve regularly, bringing Holy Communion and saying the rosary with him.

On one occasion, I invited a Maryknoll missionary priest to bring Holy Communion to Steve. This missionary had just returned from Tasmania, where he had lived for forty years. Before being given the Blessed Sacrament, Steve asked the priest these questions:

"Father, you have seen hundreds die. What is it like when they come close to the end?"

"Who fights it? Who welcomes it? What do you think happens to our bodies?"

"Where do we go? How many deaths are peaceful?"

Rather than answer Steve's questions, Father told him about a man named Yong, who was so weak from AIDS that he hadn't left his mud hut in Tasmania for three years. The villagers placed his straw bed under a tree, so he could die a peaceful death. This man had nothing; yet he had everything. He had community, caretakers, and a comfortable place to die—under a tree.

I was aware of the importance of community and caretakers, so I encouraged others to participate. A neighbor brought meals; others sent cards, wrote letters and prayed. That's what others did. I knew what I could do: invite others to pray with me for Steve.

Steve acquiesced to my hosting a prayer group, provided that we say the rosary. Our time of prayer gave way to times of fellowship—we drank *fumé blanc*, indulged in squash soup with crabmeat, and finished off with Mint Milano Pepperidge Farm cookies. Some of us sat on my Sarouk rug that I bought at auction in New York in the 1970s, thinking it was so extravagant. Others perched on my antique chairs from the Red Shed in Mystic, Connecticut, where I squeezed grocery money from my budget, so as to give Helen Gill, the owner, a deposit. Steve gasped with delight when he walked into the living room. I was thrilled that the environment I worked so hard to create was one that he appreciated. The city lights spread across the black January sky dazzled him. Most important, God was present in my living room that night—with people I didn't know three years before (and half of them not until an hour before)—discussing questions I'd not even asked my family. Steve cut to the chase.

"Why are we on earth?"

"How should I spend the time I have left?"

"Where will I go when I die?"

Steve wasn't expecting answers. He just had to ask the questions. That was part of his process of preparing for death. We get so caught up in the mundane: What will I have for dinner? How will I get everything done? Who should I invite to my party? If this group had met at a social event, we would have been grasping for words, frightened by his questions. But there we were, strangers fielding the big questions of life. When we asked Steve what he needed, he responded, "prayer, prayer, prayer," and then we concluded with the Rosary.

The Rosary. I said it on the bus en route to my memoir class at the University of Washington. I said it walking down the hill on my way to work. And I said it as I fell asleep.

When Steve was at Swedish Hospital for chemo treatments, I would walk the three blocks from my apartment to visit him after work. My initial visit to the Oncology Unit there found him curled up in the fetal position, his face glistening with perspiration. He was writhing from pain and asked me to take his hand.

"Helen, I don't think I want to live anymore. My body can't endure this."

This man was inviting me to enter a zone of his life that he reserved for few people. He needed someone to hold on to. So, I reached out to his sweaty hand, with my dry arthritic hand. He held on to me the way my toddler children had clung to me when I took them into the ocean on Rhode Island's coast. If I loosened my grip, the breakers would have swept them out to sea. I did not let that happen to my children. I would not let that happen to Steve.

At the same time the cautious side of me was shouting not to mislead Steve and encourage a relationship that couldn't go anywhere. He was seventeen years younger than I was; he was gay. Besides, I reasoned, he was opinionated and outshined me intellectually. Fat chance that I'd have in winning any arguments! But there was a side of Steve that was compassionate and thoughtful. He considered this prognosis an opportunity to minister to the terminally ill. "I can help raise up others through acts of kindness and forgiveness," he said.

Those acts of kindness revealed themselves in countless ways. Rather than investing energy in feeling sorry for himself, he ministered to people; he ministered to his garden. The first Sunday after Steve was discharged from the hospital, he attended Mass. There he encountered a man who appeared to be down on his luck. It turned out that he, too, had pancreatic cancer, and he was estranged from his family. Steve was all ears as he listened to this man's story. They met weekly, until Steve no longer had the energy.

When one of his neighbors was diagnosed with breast cancer, Steve accompanied her to the doctor. She would often answer the phone when I called Steve at home. Although we never met, I felt that we had bonded over our shared friendship with Steve.

Just as he ministered to people at St. James and his neighbors, he also treated his garden with tenderness. When he was too weak to cultivate his garden, others served as co-gardeners. On Good Friday, Todd, a fellow parishioner, moved boulders in Steve's garden so that Steve could plant perennials. I thought of the angel who, on Easter Sunday, rolled back the stone of the tomb where Christ was buried. What boulders needed to be removed from my life to make way for new growth?

Steve also had a way of lifting my spirits when they most needed it. One night after a particularly stressful day at work, I slid the key into my apartment lock at 7:00 p.m., ready for some rest and relaxation. I poured a glass of Chardonnay, lit a candle, put on Mozart's flute concerto, and heated up yesterday's shrimp casserole. Then I called Steve.

"Oh, Helen, it's you!"

"Steve, I don't want to tire you. Are you able to talk?"

"Talking to you is like digesting a delicious meal."

"Oh, what a lovely thing to say."

Did he know that I was blushing? Such irony. I was supposed to cheer him up. He was the fellow with pancreatic cancer; I'm just a weary geriatric divorcee working to pay my rent. I was healthy, and he was dying. I took off my shoes, put my bare feet on the glass coffee table, and poured another Chardonnay. Then I replaced Mozart with Sarah Vaughan's "Embraceable You."

"So, tell me what you had for dinner, Steve."

"Ground beef patties, mashed potatoes and mushroom gravy—dull and Midwestern. But I wallow in this cuisine, as if I am in a five-star Parisian restaurant. Helen, when I look at my mortality, I see a beauty in the commonplace that I never saw before. Every moment is grace. Life is a matter of divestiture—a divine calculus, or the satisfaction of basement cleaning, garden weeding, and meat and potatoes, too."

Steve, a Latin scholar, winner of the Chelsea Garden Show, student of Dante and Aristotle—mashed potatoes and gravy? Five minutes pass, one hour. . . . Time stood still when I was absorbed in conversation with Steve. I forgot what it was like to be 72 and working full time. This was as exciting as taking a Mediterranean cruise or playing golf in Florida. I felt a surge of energy that I thought was reserved for youths. He said my voice was warm, soothing, and gracious. The compliments he gave me were not meant to flatter. Steve was too authentic for flattery. I did see myself in a different way because of how Steve viewed me, and I wondered, was I in love?

Part of the glue that bound us together was the fact that we had both traversed a circuitous and rugged life path. Steve viewed himself as a St. Augustine or a St. Paul—someone who had "sown his oats" and, like Paul, had been struck by lightning. Likewise, there are things in my past that I'd like to erase—my addictions, the ways I've hurt or disappointed others, my insistence on getting my way. Nevertheless, God was holding my hand while I negotiated the peaks and valleys of divorce, job loss, illness, and the challenges of raising and educating three teenagers without bouncing any checks.

The night before I flew to Chicago for my niece's wedding, I visited Steve at the hospital, where he had been readmitted for an infusion. He expected to go home the next day, for his old energy was coming back. Personally, I was running on empty, because I had put in a ten-hour day at work, gone to Mass, and needed to pack.

The next morning the phone rang as I was leaving for the airport. It was Steve.

"Helen, they pumped volumes of blood from my lung. I have a pulmonary embolism."

"Oh, my gosh! How frightening! I'd be right over if I didn't have to leave for the airport. I'll call you when I return on Tuesday. Know that I'll be praying for you, Steve. My rosary is in my pocket."

When I returned home the next week the red light, indicating that I had three messages, was flashing on my home phone. All were variations of a message saying that Steve had died. This reminded me of a time too near, when my sister Peggy called to tell me of the inoperable pancreatic cancer that would brutally seize her life, too. I cried so hard then that I called my doctor to see if she could prescribe an anti-crying pill. She didn't have any then. She didn't have any this time, either. I telephoned my boss to say I wouldn't be in. I knew that I'd be worthless in my current state, even though I didn't tell him that.

One of the three messages about Steve's death included a request from Sister Anne at St. James, asking if I would be one of the readers for his funeral. Oh, my, I wondered if I would be able to hold myself together for that! But of course, I had to say yes. What a privilege!

From the pulpit of St. James Cathedral, I looked out on the mourners as I read from the *Book of Wisdom.* They included classicists, scholars, seminarians, a woman in remission from breast cancer, gays, straights, gardeners, landscape architects, lawyers, recovering alcoholics. The mortar holding us together was losing Steve. Four years ago, I did not know this man, or these mourners.

Father Ryan's homily was made to order for Steve.

"Steve knew that the sufferings of the present life were as nothing compared to the glory to come, and that knowledge kept his eyes and his heart fixed on the prize of eternal life and joy unending."

Oh, my, he really did live those words!

Thankfully, I listened to Steve's (and God's) voice, instead of playing those old tapes of caution, fear, and propriety. I can't imagine missing the intimate conversations, the challenging arguments, and the opportunity to comfort him and learn how to prepare for *my* final journey. I am all the richer for having had that experience, painful as it was to watch this dear man suffer and die. Steve taught me how to respect time, what comprises a friend, and the value of suffering. From him I also learned that illness and death can be purifying, ennobling, and even an occasion for creating community. And I learned that I did not need to give the sadness of life the power to define me. That is not to say that I didn't need additional support. I went to grief counseling, wrote daily reflections in my journal, and made no effort to hold back my tears.

Through my friendship with Steve and walking beside him on his journey toward death, I'm more confident, I'm humbler, and I'm more vulnerable. No man in my life has ever showered me with the spray of compliments Steve sent my way. He liked the way I presented myself, he liked my voice, and he liked visiting with me over the phone. When I told him that a Jesuit said I needed to work on humility, Steve alluded to St. Augustine, noting that this third-century saint believed that "humility is the basis of all virtue."

The gifted spiritual writer Ron Rolheiser maintains that to be earthy means to "keep your shoes off before the burning bush," as Moses did. He contends that to be humble is to know your limits and your vulnerability. This was the message from the Jesuit who admonished me. Steve was saying the same thing to me in companionship. No one can take off their shoes without feeling vulnerable. As Alan Worfelt, a grief counselor, affirmed, "that doesn't mean I can't thrive again in a new form and in a new way." And that has been happening ever since I encountered Steve on the corner of Marion and Terry that night outside St. James Cathedral.

REFLECTION AND JOURNALING

By weeping we dispense our wrath, and tears go through the heart, even like a stream.

—Ovid

- When have you been surprised by your feelings upon losing someone whom you have not known long and only from afar?
- How did you work through that grief?
- Who offered support to you? (sometimes the least likely person)
- What qualities did that person have that brought comfort to you?

CHAPTER NINE

Miss Mary

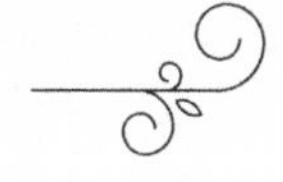

For healing and spiritual wholeness lie only in the future – the ever-present future that unfolds before us.

—R. Scott Sullender

She was "dressed to the nines," as if she were dining at Seattle's premier restaurant. She cut his meat, held the cranberry juice to his lips, and scooped applesauce into his mouth after the nurse ground up his pills so he could swallow them. It was Mary and George Martin's ritual at the Memory Support wing of Horizon House, Seattle's foremost retirement community. Because Mary could no longer care for her husband, George, she had moved him to this unit for nursing care. After George had dinner, Mary would join her friends in the facility's dining room for the residents who could still live alone in their apartments.

Mary and George moved to Horizon House from their Seattle waterfront home at the urging of their daughter Marion. Her parents' fragile health was a concern, but so was her own. Marion joined them at Horizon House because at age 52, she had end-stage breast cancer. Mary and George visited Marion in the Health Center every day. Then, while she had the strength, Marion would go to her parents' apartment at Horizon House, where the three of them would have tea parties, replete with Mary's finest china and linens. Fresh flowers were a given.

Marion told her one sibling, DeDe, who lives in Houston, Texas, that when things got bad, she would let her know. "I've lived all my life in Seattle, where I grew up and where Mother and Daddy live now. I'll call you when I need you." Meanwhile, DeDe regularly went to the gym to strengthen her muscles so she could carry Marion anywhere, if necessary. "I didn't know how she'd need me, but I figured she'd need me strong." Often DeDe would anxiously call her mother to see if it was time to come to be with her sister. Mary told DeDe, "No, not until the expectation that Marion would not live through the night." When that time came, DeDe said, "I sat with Marion the last days and nights of her life. She was medicated and unconscious." Now it was Mary's turn to take care of George.

Spoon-feeding a man who was once Boeing's chief engineer and expert in the structural design of B-17 and B-29 bombers, Mary felt she was being strong for George. Somehow, it was as important as hosting their legendary parties for Seattle's power brokers, her gracious manners and warm smile endearing her to all at a swath of gatherings across the continent, including embassy parties in Washington, DC.

"Those were the days," she said wistfully describing her elegant show-stopper gowns. But there was another side to Mary. Boeing Management expected engineers' wives to be leaders in the city's arts and educational and health organizations. Mary took this directive seriously. She was a founding member of the Seattle Opera Association and served on the boards of the Seattle Children's Theatre, Seattle Symphony, Museum of History & Industry, and the Seattle Art Museum. As Director of Philanthropy at Horizon House, I was in awe of all that she had contributed to Seattle's culture. She simply thought this was what George's wife should do, as ordinary as getting dinner on the table.

Now she was creating a steady island of calm in the Memory Support wing, which harbored resilient seniors from the Greatest Generation who had managed to weather the Great Depression and World War II. The least I could do was visit them after I spent a day of writing appeals and acknowledgments. I would "table hop" in the resident dining room, engaging these frail heroes in storytelling. Even though he was not able to respond verbally to her, the tenderness and devotion between Mary and George spoke volumes. They were both divested of so much that had defined them, but they were in a passageway of something much larger. Mary often asked me to join them in this passageway, and thus began friendships with Mary, her daughter, and her granddaughter. What a gift to be given a window into the lives we pass every day!

George was soon transferred to the skilled nursing unit, so I wasn't surprised to see his photo and obituary on the "Passings Board" in the lobby at Horizon House. The next week I saw Mary walking into the dining room while holding on to another resident. When Mary saw me, she said in her soft voice, "Helen, I'm losing my balance and my sight since I lost George." A few days later, while heading to a meeting with my boss, I got a glimpse of Mary lying on the lobby floor. She had fallen while getting out of the elevator. I rushed over to her and knelt down beside her.

"I had a dizzy spell, Helen," she whispered.

"Mrs. Martin," said Lauri, Director of Health Services, "you need to go to the hospital. We want to be sure it is nothing more serious."

"I've never been in a hospital in my life; I don't intend to go now!"

"Mary," I said, "Lauri knows what's best. You don't want to put yourself at risk."

"I will only go if Helen accompanies me," she said with a look of determination that she must have reserved for meetings of the Opera Guild.

When I glanced at Lauri to glean her reaction, she nodded, and I asked her to explain to my boss why I would not be at our meeting. Then I climbed into the ambulance with my precious cargo. Lauri called Mary's granddaughter, Sarah, telling her that I would stay with Mary until she arrived. As we sat in the Emergency Room, Mary spoke of how she missed George and how life had lost its meaning. She asked about me. She hung on my every word, as if I was the most important person in the world. I hung on Mary's words, too. Why? After all, Mary was one of over 400 residents at Horizon House. I had never gone to the hospital with any of them. Why her? There was an elegant gentility that drew me to her; but more than that, I was touched by her sweetness and courage all wrapped into one package. Here she was, having just survived the loss of her daughter and husband. Now she was coming to the end of her own life. What a gift to accompany her on that path, along with DeDe, Sarah, and the many others who were the most important people in her life.

Mary came home after a series of tests and appeared stable. When DeDe learned of Mary's fall, she flew to Seattle from Houston, and Mary invited me to have dinner with them the next night; she wanted me to get to know DeDe. It seemed that I was being woven tighter and tighter into the tapestry of Mary's life, as if I had been waiting for her to pick up some of my dropped stitches. Mary shared, "Helen, I am so glad you can be with us for dinner tomorrow. Helena Harper will join us. She is lovely. I know she will enjoy you." Helena had her second leg amputated several weeks before.

DeDe had extended her stay to celebrate her mother's birthday. On my lunch hour, I picked up a bouquet of daffodils and a card. As I was entering Horizon House with the flowers, I saw Mary and DeDe on a bench next to the entrance. I handed Mary her birthday card. A long fold-out in purple, it had a star-filled crescent moon dropping stars. Inside were these words:

"Surely a star danced in heaven on the day you were born."

"DeDe, would you read it for me, please?" said Mary. I had forgotten that Mary had glaucoma.

As DeDe read it, she was overcome with emotion. She began crying (as I did, too).

"Helen, you are the dearest friend I have ever had," emoted Mary.

"Mary, I know there is a long line of people who call themselves your dearest friends."

"None of them would have gone in an ambulance on a bumpy road with an old lady like me! I will never forget what you did that day!"

The next week Mary fell at the bathroom sink, hitting her head on the bathtub. This time there was no question about an ambulance. When I called Mary at the hospital, her medicated voice whispered that it didn't seem right that I wasn't with her. I cancelled my luncheon plans and went to the hospital. There she was, puffy eyes and swollen face with tomato soup encrusted on her hospital gown. Mary apologized for how she looked. I said, "Mary, all I see are your beautiful eyes, your smile, and your grace."

Mary returned to Horizon House saying how lucky she was not to have broken her back or neck. She agreed that it was time to move to the Assisted Living section there. DeDe and the housekeeping staff managed to make a swift transition. When I went in to see Mary, I expected a hospital bed and a few chairs—standard fare for end-of-life facilities. Not so for the ever-elegant Mary. Her new space was right out of *Antiques Magazine*. There was the Chippendale chair from Davis's antiques on Fifth Avenue. (Mary was one of the first of her crowd to collect antiques, and Mr. Davis was a superb teacher.) There was her music cabinet. There was a Royal Crown Derby dish (just like mine!) on the coffee table, next to a picture of George. To top it off, quite literally, over her bed were two antique bronze and crystal sconces bought at Gumps in San Francisco, while traveling with George.

On her dresser was a Steuben vase that George had eyed at Steuben's in New York over fifty years earlier. George hand-carried this treasure on the entire flight from New York to Seattle. When he arrived home, it was tucked under his overcoat, and Mary gasped when he presented her with this surprise anniversary gift. There was not an item in her new apartment that did not have a story behind it. I was especially drawn to the eighteenth-century music stand with an Andrew Wyatt book gifted to Mary and George by Marion many Christmases ago. Items that completed this jewel of a room were a needlepoint chair and footstool made by Mary's grandmother.

DeDe, with the help of a decorator, managed to orchestrate this entire process, for Mary's vision had taken a free fall due to macular degeneration and glaucoma. Nevertheless, she was clear as to what she wanted. "I don't want a bedroom," Mary ordered. "I want a sitting room!"

DeDe waxed nostalgic: "Mother has been surrounded by beauty all of her life. We have always had homes with beautiful antiques, art works, and gardens. There is no reason why she needs to give that up. This is all part of her transition." She certainly didn't yield to a sterile medical environment; DeDe ensured that Mary was surrounded by beauty. Nor did she give up her *joie de vivre.*

The next morning Mary greeted me in a blue jumpsuit.

"Mary, you look like a teenager trying out for the track team."

"So, let's make a dash, Helen!"

She climbed into bed and told me of the tiring, but exciting afternoon she and DeDe had with the decorator, who helped her select her bathroom wallpaper.

"Helen, you won't believe this, but I have frogs in my bathroom! The paper is a soft yellow with green frogs all over. I may even have them on the ceiling. I wish you could see it! Heck, if I can't be a bit 'fey' at my age, when can I?"

When I said goodbye, I squeezed her hand and kissed her on the forehead. I think if my mother had lived to be an elderly woman, she would have been like Mary. Is that why I'm being woven into her tapestry? Or is she being woven into mine? Whichever the case, this is an opportunity to participate in the most important journey humans take. She was sprinting for the finish in her blue jumpsuit.

The next day I tapped on Mary's door with a bouquet of white and pink flowers. DeDe was sitting on the floral chintz loveseat, reading Mary Oliver's poetry. "Mother is asleep, but come in. Helen; they are gorgeous!"

"Mother, Helen is here," said DeDe.

Mary opened her eyes, and DeDe described the flowers.

"Mother, they are white and pink lilies, hydrangeas, and rhododendron. The hydrangeas have touches of the same pink as the rhododendron. It is so delicate; it is just perfect."

"Mary, of all the ones I saw at the market, this one had your name on it." I put it up to her face so that she could smell and touch the flowers.

"Oh, Helen. I love you so much."

When I tip-toed into her dark room the next week, I saw a beautiful woman with a finely chiseled face, mouth wide open, breathing swiftly. My father would have called her a "classic beauty." She had deep blue eyes, pink, round cheeks, and an aquiline nose. She was like a grown-up Hummel figurine.

"Mary, I want you to know that I've been thinking about you and praying for you."

"I know, Helen. That means so much. We must get together soon. I've just not been myself."

As I walked toward the elevator, I saw DeDe talking to the case manager, who told her that it was time for Mary to go into Hospice. DeDe tearfully embraced me.

"Three of my family members will have died here," she said. DeDe then shared the fact that she had breast cancer. Shivers went up and down my spine as I thought of Mary having two daughters with breast cancer, one of whom had died from it. "I think the hardest thing I ever did is tell my parents that news," reflected DeDe.

At lunch time the next day, I went up to see Mary. DeDe was sitting with her.

"Mother doesn't see much reason to live; she has had so much loss." I looked at Mary, who was lying flat on her back, smiling at me. A stillness echoed in the room.

"Helen, there has been George, Marion, and then DeDe's diagnosis, which devastated me."

"Mary, that is a lot of loss. And then there is your vision, your energy, and your mobility. It doesn't make any sense, does it Mary?"

"The minute we expect it to make sense, we are in trouble," chimed in DeDe. "Nor should we compare our lives to others'. It is simply life. It is unfair and always has been. Our bodies are decaying, and the only thing that is left is our spirit, and that will go on forever. Some day we may have answers, when we look down and see why it happened." It was clear that the Martin women were not letting the harsh headwinds of life do them in.

I told Mary that she reminded me of what my mother would have been like in her nineties. When I revealed that my mother died when I was sixteen, she said, "I'm sorry, Helen. That is too young to lose your mother." She spoke the truth. I missed so much by not having a Mom as I traversed the milestones from teenager to young adult.

Mary went on. "We're living too long. But then I think living this long has taught me so much. When my father died, I told my family that I was pregnant. Their expressions changed from ones of grief to ones of hope. Life goes on; we grow old and die and leave the world to the next generation." I told her about my visit to the salmon hatchery and how the salmon struggle to go upstream to lay their eggs before they die.

The next day on my lunch hour I stopped in to see Mary. I gently knocked on the door, for I didn't want to awaken her.

"Come in!" There was DeDe, sketching.

"She is asleep, Helen, but you can wake her up."

"Oh, Helen, how are you? What have you been doing?" said Mary, as she opened her eyes.

"Mary, you have a perpetual smile on your face. I think you were born with that smile!"

DeDe was doing a drawing of Asiatic lilies at all different stages of development—from buds, just opening, to those in full bloom. "We all bloom at different stages of life, Helen," said DeDe.

I thought of the late Henri J. M. Nouwen, the Dutch theologian, who believed that the most important thing that we can do is to listen to people's stories. Then we need to tell our own and let them know with words, handshakes, and hugs that you do not simply like them, but you truly love them. That is what was happening in Room 305 in Assisted Living at Horizon House.

DeDe, Mary, and Sarah were going to meet with the doctor to be sure that there was clarity around Mary's situation.

"Mother told the doctor she wants to die. I told her that the doctor needs to hear her wishes. It is her life."

There was an enveloping sense of unity in the room as I reflected on the honesty with which the Martin women faced death—so unlike the way my family did in the 1940s when we knew no other way than to pretend that it wasn't happening. The next day I encountered DeDe and Sarah in the lobby. "She's on a journey, Helen," said DeDe. I asked her when a good time to visit was. DeDe suggested mealtime, when Mary would have more energy. DeDe said, "She may choose not to eat, and I told her it was okay: 'Mom, you are entitled to do whatever you want to do. You have earned that right after 94 years!'"

Mary smiled at me, lifted her hand up, and stroked my head. I stayed only a few moments, for her energy was flagging.

When I saw DeDe's number on caller ID, I knew that Mary had joined George and Marion. DeDe sounded calm and relieved that her mother was at peace. She asked me to serve as a greeter at the memorial service at Horizon House. Black-attired ladies and gentlemen came in one after another. These were the leaders and founders of arts organizations, schools, and hospitals. But more important, they were mourners. DeDe read from Mary Oliver and T. S. Eliot. There was a video that revealed Mary and George as a loving couple. All was done with grace, dignity, and class—just like Mary. I felt a sense of sweet times lost that could never be reclaimed.

The next August DeDe was in town for Wagner's *Ring* series at the Seattle Opera. An opera lover like her parents, she relished this time. Horizon House represented loss for her, so we had lunch at the Frye Museum, instead. DeDe handed me Mary Oliver's *Thirst*. Inscribed was this message: "For Helen, for all the time and love you have shared with Mother and with the family...I thank you. Blessings, Love, DeDe."

I could talk to DeDe forever. She shared, "Our souls choose our families and teach us lessons our souls need to learn. We were not brought into this world to be unhappy. Part of it is finding a way to dance. I watched you with my mother. You still have to grieve *your* mother." We stood in the sunlit patio of the Frye Museum, and DeDe blessed me with healing light. I promised I would address that sadness. Then we walked out into the sunlight, and I realized why Mary was so eager to have me meet DeDe.

REFLECTION AND JOURNALING

What is important for us to recognize is that Mother's own life invites us to see her death as a death that can bring us not only grief, but also joy, not only pain, but also healing, not only the experience of having lost but also the experience of having found.

—Henri J. M. Nouwen

- Mary and George were not spared the pain of loss. George's illness, Mary's vision challenges, the death of their daughter Marion, and DeDe's cancer diagnosis were more than most people have to endure in a lifetime. What have you learned from the losses you've experienced?
- The importance of beauty in Mary's life was apparent. Her appreciation of her physical surroundings, poetry, music, and her collections were a few examples. What are ways these were represented in her Memorial Service?
- How do you want to be remembered at your funeral?

CHAPTER TEN

Rose

Grief is not a disorder, a disease or a sign of weakness.
It is an emotional, physical and spiritual necessity, the price you pay for love.
The only cure for grief is to grieve.
—Earl Grollman

It took Rose five minutes to reach the door. I could hear her saying, "I'm coming, I'm coming. Helen! I'm sorry it takes me so long. You don't want to visit with me. I'm a mess."

As I stood in front of Apartment 13A, I thought of the implications of the words seeping through the door. This was someone whose eyes were her window to the world—the world of books, movies, and opera. Losing her sight was devastating for Rose, a subscriber to the *New Yorker* and the daily *New York Times.* She couldn't even read the letters her grandsons Lee and Alan sent her from college. While I waited for Rose to "feel" her way through the bedroom, down the serpentine hallway, and into the living room, I said a prayer to St. Lucy, the fourth-century martyr who was the patron saint of the blind. "Please perform a miracle and bring the light back to Rose's eyes," I whispered.

Rose was my neighbor at Panorama House on Seattle's First Hill. I had noticed her in the lobby with Shirley and Joan, with whom she regularly embarked on a cultural odyssey. These treks were to *La Traviata* at the

Seattle Opera, *Heartbreak House* at the Intiman Theatre, or Brahms's *Second Symphony* at Benaroya Hall. One night I noticed that Rose was fumbling with her keys and running her hand over the door's surface, desperate to find the doorknob. I asked if I could help her. "Oh, I would so appreciate that, Helen. I've been having visual challenges." I told her that I understood, for I had glaucoma.

Rose was the only tenant I knew on my floor. The rest were like ships passing in the night going into separate ports of call, not knowing who was on board or in what direction they were headed. Behind those doors were people with jobs, families, and passions. One rainy February Sunday, I invited them all to my apartment, 13B, hoping that a Merlot or Chardonnay would loosen their tongues enough so they would share their stories. As I listened to their tales, I thought of the Native Americans and their pow-wows. There was a pow-wow of elders around my glass coffee table, and there was plenty of smoke. Rose's story set us all on fire.

She spoke of her job as a researcher for the New York Psychiatric Institute until her retirement at 80, eight years prior. Rose was also a devotee of music, theatre, ballet, and art. She shared these loves with her late husband and first love, Richard Bender, an arranger for WOR Radio and fan of Broadway shows. When Richard died, Rose remained in their home in Queens, New York, until she fell down the stairs and broke her arm. Then her daughter, Beth, who lived in Seattle with her physician husband, Mark, and two sons, urged her to move. She made a good life for herself in Seattle. She made my life a good one, too, teaching me that one is never too old to learn, that it is okay to fail, and that it's *not* okay to give up on life, no matter what the hardship. Love is what matters. Every day presents an opportunity for that.

One day Rose invited me for tea. We discussed politics. We discussed religion. We discussed family. We discussed human rights. She shared my indignation over that morning's *New York Times* exposé on the prevalence of corporal punishment in the public schools. She called the reporter who wrote the article and told him that "such a backward approach was the last way to stimulate thinking and interest in the subject being taught. Furthermore, it could leave indelible emotional scars." From then on, I wouldn't consider submitting a letter or op-ed piece to the *Seattle Times* without Rose, my personal editor-in-chief, signing off. Her insights and insistence on clarity and accuracy helped me hone my writing skills. It seemed that her growing physical vulnerability strengthened her resolve to make the most of her gifts of wisdom, insight, and intelligence. She was tapping into the reserves that had accumulated in her life's treasury.

Rose was a child of the Great Depression—the middle child of a Russian emigrant from Bucharest, Romania, with an older brother and younger sister. Her father managed a moving and storage company, and he and Rose's mother, a native of Kiev, Ukraine, raised their children in a two-family house in Brooklyn. The Depression meant managing on a smaller income and spending less. Allowances were cut and movies were no longer an option. Rose's mother made all of Rose's and her sister's clothes, and the summer and winter curtains, while her father learned how to install a roof and fix a toilet. These habits of persistence and hard work were etched into their children, and the money saved went toward their education and music lessons.

A commitment to education and the arts was a thread that ran through the tapestry of Rose's family history. Her brother's violin lessons continued while he attended college at night and worked in the Garment District during the day. Rose entered Hunter College at sixteen, skipping fifth and ninth grades. "I walked eight blocks to the trolley at the Church Avenue Station, where I got the Eighth Avenue subway. It was brand new, and I could smell the fresh paint on the wicker seats. Then I'd transfer to the A-train on Fifty-Ninth Street and ride that to Two Hundred Thirty-Eighth Street."

Sigmund Freud must have had Rose and her husband, Richard, in mind when he said that love and work are the cornerstones of our humanity. Rose and Richard's priority was their family, and Rose did not work full time until the children were in school. It is not surprising that they raised three intelligent, dedicated, and compassionate individuals. Their daughter, Beth, is a social worker and Director of Social Services at The Summit, a retirement community in Seattle. Their son Eric teaches English in the Bronx Public Schools, and their son Mark is a lawyer in New York. It occurred to me that Rose would have been a superb Supreme Court Justice, for she always had an intelligent opinion or insight of her own to pass on.

In her dotage, her mind was as active as ever, despite her visual challenges and lack of access to television, newspapers, books, or movies. Even though her sight may have been challenged, her passion for learning was intact. "She has a way of bringing things to a whole different level," said her friend Shirley. "When we went to the opera, movies, or theatre, it's as if Rosie was inside the artist's soul."

One Saturday when I called Rose, I heard voices in the background. "Oh, Rose, I think you have company. I'll call you back."

"Oh, no, Helen dear, I'm listening to the Metropolitan Opera on radio. This is a regular Saturday morning occurrence for me, and today I'm tuned in to Verdi's *Simon Boccanegra.*

In addition to being current with arts and the news, Rose was continually expressing her views on religion and philosophy. One day I asked her if she believed in God.

She commented, "Helen, I'm a spiritual person, but I don't believe in God. The world, in terms of religious and spiritual thinking, is man-made. Basically, people are good. Look at the outpouring of philanthropy and compassion in the wake of the Haiti earthquake! But it is those who manipulate the good people for the sake of power or money who have done the greatest harm."

It seemed inevitable that our discussion would turn to the Holocaust—a subject that always sent shivers up and down my spine. I asked Rose if she had family members who perished during that dark time in Europe's history. "They had all immigrated before the 1930s, as did my husband's father, who came to the United States in 1901. Unfortunately, his eight brothers and sisters remained in Prague, where they owned a major department store. His was a prosperous middle-class family, living in a villa with servants. The family knew that trouble was brewing. But they had so much to deal with if they closed the store, such as meeting with their creditors and making arrangements with the banks. Frantic letters describing the chaos in Prague traversed the Atlantic. But it was too late. In 1938 the Nazis took them all off to Auschwitz, where they perished. It didn't matter that they were educated and had a classical pianist among them."

"I understand why you question God's existence," I said. "Have you read the Old Testament?"

I told her about King David's lament psalms, which were so comforting when I went through my divorce and when my sister Peggy died. Then I read Psalm 13.

How long, Lord? Will you utterly forget me?
How long will you hide your face from me?
How long must I carry sorrow in my soul,
grief in my heart day after day?
How long will my enemy triumph over me?

Then I shared St. Mark's Gospel in which he relates how Christ cured a blind man by rubbing sputum with soil on the man's eyes.

"I'll pray that Christ will cure your blindness, Rose."

"If He does, you've got a convert," she replied with a giggle.

We both agreed that we shared our core values–that we're just taking different paths.

One day I missed the *New York Times,* and I knocked on Rose's door to see if she had saved hers. It took her a while to answer. This dignified lady, usually beautifully coiffed and attired in *haute couture*, stood in front of me in her pajamas. "Helen, I cancelled my subscription. I can't read anymore. In fact, I can barely see you!" She had gone to a foreign film with Shirley and Joan and asked them why there were no subtitles. "There *are* subtitles, Rosie," was their response. The next day she was in her ophthalmologist's office. He gave her injections hoping that within three weeks there might be some improvement.

Rose's family was concerned about how her visual challenges compromised her ability to function in her apartment. Difficult though it was, Rose knew that moving to The Summit, an assisted living facility, would be the prudent thing to do. There she would have people checking in on her and preparing her meals. I assured her that I would visit her, for The Summit was across the street from Panorama House. I said, "Rose, I won't give you up just because you're across the street!"

After she had had time to unpack, I gave her a call, thinking I'd stop by for a short visit.

"Oh, Helen dear, I have a date this afternoon. After lunch, Bernie, a gentleman who shares my dining with me, is coming in to read me the *New York Times*. I need to know what is happening every day, all over the world! I don't like to live in a circumscribed world of my own isolation. That is mental death."

Rose told me that she had always felt that we were connected. This affinity was particularly apparent when Rose reflected eloquently on different occasions about philosophy or art. "There are biological forces that enable us to be creative people. Some of the creative products of our own efforts are writing, painting, sculpting, teaching, acting, music playing, and healing arts. Children are the finest gifts that we make while we're alive. These are the things that stand in our stead when we are no longer here to contribute to making the world a better place."

Rose's failing vision didn't interfere with her agenda to make the world a better place. I thought of fortitude, one of the four cardinal virtues that I learned from the nuns in parochial school. Fortitude denotes courage, but it is a conscious courage that is reasoned. Rose deserved the Olympic Gold Medal for that. She did admit, however, that the "golden years" were not gold at all. "It's all about loss. Loss of physical faculties, loss of friends, loss of control. This is especially hard for someone like me who likes to be in charge," she said.

Rose went on to explain that her body was at a stage in which she no longer had control. "It simply doesn't do what I want it to do." She was quite philosophical about the fact that she had been healthy until she was 90. Then her vision failed. "But all other systems seem to be working. The digestive system. The cardiovascular system. My kidneys and bladder are functioning."

My, this woman is a tower of strength, I mused. Will I have the courage to accept my physical limitations and vulnerability with such grace?

"Oh, Rose, you have such a healthy attitude. You view your body as if you were doing research at the New York Psychiatric Institute. What resilience and lack of self-pity you exhibit!"

Rose responded, "For all of these years, when I've faced a problem, I analyzed it, came up with a solution and lived it. That's how we resolved family problems and had harmony in our family."

She insisted that physical diminishments weren't a thermometer of her happiness. "I have a treasury that is irreplaceable. It is my family and friends, like you and Joan and Shirley, who nourish my spirit. Besides, when things get too bad physically, I pretend that I'm Eleanor Roosevelt, who said, "When you are sitting in the dark, you get up and light a candle." We reminisced about Eleanor's challenges: her rejection by her mother, her father's death, her lonely childhood, and her husband, Franklin's, infidelity. Rather than defeating her, those losses were a catalyst that strengthened her resolve. Eleanor enhanced the status of working women, was a delegate to the United Nations General Assembly, chaired the committee that drafted the Universal Declaration of Human Rights, and, during the Kennedy administration, chaired the Committee on the Status of Women.

I reminded Rose of the legacy that *she* had passed on to her grandsons. Lee is working in science and producing artificial limbs for disabled people. His brother, Alan, devotes his efforts to a company that develops green approaches to heating homes. Both the boys credit their passion for social justice and the environment to their grandmother. Lee's altruistic spirit inspired him to go to Morocco as a volunteer.

"As laudable as his volunteer service was," Rose commented about her grandson, "these small Middle Eastern nations are so vulnerable. One can be held for ransom, with no diplomatic recourse. I am well aware of the dangers, with an inadequate police force and an unstable government. But he is so enthused and thinks only of the positive and adventurous aspects of the trip. The last thing that occurs to him is the possibility of violence, and I wasn't about to discourage him."

Despite her visual challenges, Rose was able to help me edit my writing. I was especially grateful for her feedback on my life story. "You showed such courage," was Rose's reaction to my sharing especially painful times of my life: my mother's death, when I was sixteen, the challenges I faced while living in New York as a young single woman, and my marriage and divorce. "You were such a risk-taker!" she commented. I told her of my mistakes and missed opportunities, and the ways in which I had hurt people, including my late husband. I shared with her the chapter in which I apologized to my husband for not being the wife that he needed. I thanked him for all that he had taught me and given me, especially our three gifted children. When his health failed, I placed him in a nursing home in Florida and helped care for him in his final days, thirty years after I had left him. I was touched by Rose's comments:

"You realized that divorce was a choice you had to make for your own and your children's benefit. Difficult though it was, you did not involve the children in your conflicts. Rather, you developed a plan of healing. That is extraordinary. A lot of people can't get through the first stage. They would rather hate forever than say they are sorry." When I told her how grateful I was for her "editing," she said there is nothing more important than feeling useful.

One day I received an engraved invitation to Rose's 90th birthday party. She did not hesitate to tell me what she wanted for her birthday: a Brahms piano concerto! With the CD in hand, I entered the elegant salon with Cole Porter and Ira Gershwin piano music playing in the background. There was Rose surrounded by her proud family and a room full of fans, elegant in her wine and gold brocade jacket, with a corsage of pink roses on her shoulder. One would never know that this exquisite matriarch was blind. But true to her form as an actor, she pretended that she could see her entire audience. I whispered in her ear that I was so honored to be there, and that I loved her.

Seated at my table was her friend Bernie Kessler. They still had a standing date on Saturday mornings, when he read her the *New York Times*. On the other side of me was Shirley, who told me how thrilled Rose was to participate in my writing. "Helen, when I think of you, I think of *Mitzvah*, which in Hebrew means 'we care for one another.' This is what helping you with your writing does for Rosie." I told her and Joan that it was a privilege to have the time, now that I was retired. Whenever I needed to find a steady island of calm, I put out to Rose's pier. Joan replied, "When we are busy, we miss the compass points of life."

I was scheduled to leave for New York to see my son Tom perform in a jazz competition as first trumpet. Before departing, I wanted to check in with Rose. It seemed that her fragile life changed every day.

She shared, "There is a dark cloud in front of me. Before I saw separate clouds, but now it is as if none of them are delineated. I am losing ambition, drive, and energy."

Oh, my, this was so unlike Rosie. I thought she was about to knock on heaven's door.

When I returned from New York, I found Rose in better spirits. She was using a walker, for there was concern about her bumping into things and having another fall. As usual, she made the best of an awkward situation. She wanted to attend the lectures and concerts but was too embarrassed to say she could not see the performers. But beautiful music had a way of buoying her spirits, so, determined, she grabbed on to her walker. "I simply correct my gait, follow the crowd, and press the lower button on the elevator wall. It's just like "Follow the Leader" that we played in grade school. I've learned to make use of other people."

"Everything is a struggle, even going to my grandniece's birthday party. I like to look at people when I talk to them. It is so uncomfortable for me to socialize under these circumstances, for you can learn so much from people's expressions." I told her that she had earned the right to do what she wanted. If she was uncomfortable going to the party, I'd come over and listen to opera tapes with her. So, that's what we did.

I worried about tiring her and always prefaced our visits with the *caveat* that we could cut this short any time. "Oh, Helen," she said, "I so look forward to our visits. They are so stimulating!"

I said, "Rose, I hope I have the kind of energy you have when I'm 91. I know people in their forties who don't have your zest for life."

"Helen, I don't want to be dead before I die," was Rose's response.

That wasn't about to happen to Rose. As I sat at her feet soaking up her wisdom, the phone rang. It was her grandson Lee, and she was absolutely ebullient when she heard his voice. "Gaga [which is what he and his brother had called Rose since they were toddlers], I want to share some exciting news with you. I am playing the oboe with an orchestra outside of San Jose!" They discussed how Verdi and Beethoven used the oboe to express sadness and joy. Then Lee hummed a melody from one of Beethoven's sonatas, and the conversation switched to the culinary arts. He told her about a chicken dish with sweet and sour sauce—a recipe from *The Joy of Cooking*—that he was serving that night. Rose told Lee how proud she was of him for his pursuit of the arts, especially those of cooking and music.

After Lee hung up Rose was so energized, that she couldn't think of anything else. "Imagine, this young man wanting to talk to his grandmother about these things. Most boys his age are so self-absorbed, the last thing they want to do is call their grandmother!" I mused that very few boys have a "Gaga" like Rose.

The next week I was hospitalized for a pacemaker implant, due to a low heart rate. When I came home, I checked my voicemail and found a message from Rose's daughter, Beth. She told me that Rose had died the previous night. It was a peaceful death and just the way Rose wanted to go—surrounded by those who loved her, with no tubes, ventilators, or respirators. She simply stopped breathing. Beth, her voice cracking, said, "Yours was an exquisite friendship!"

Rose's friend Joan told me that Bernie died three days after Rose. Her eyes welling up, Joan mused, "Rosie had a reservoir of knowledge that she continually drew on. That is what kept her going. Bernie couldn't live without her. It is difficult getting old. Rose was lucky to go the way she did. I am happy for her. Death is hard; so is birth. There is no easy way in or out."

That night I prayed that God would give me the ability to light a candle, just as Rose did, no matter how dark it was. Thank goodness I wasn't too busy to help Rose find her keys when she was entering her apartment that night. That one gesture led to a friendship that nourished me culturally, intellectually, and spiritually.

I would not have written this book if it were not for Rose encouraging me, keeping me on track, and setting a high standard. Now I am writing my reflection on *her* life. Whether etched in stone or in digital form, that narrative will be pulsing with vitality. And when I enter heaven, I suspect that Rose will be on the reception committee with her editor's pen in hand. And maybe there will be Gershwin and Cole Porter tunes as background music!

REFLECTION AND JOURNALING

It is dark now. The snow is deep blue and the ocean nearly black.
It is time for some music.

—May Sarton

- What was it about Rose that led me to reach out to her? Have you ever felt an instinct to create a connection with someone you did not know well? Describe that situation.
- Rose's guidance with Helen's writing encouraged Helen to continue crafting her memoir. What benefit did this have for Rose?
- Sharing their life stories laid the foundation for a deep friendship between Rose and Helen. Do you know someone who might like to share his or her own story?
- Rose's grandchildren played an important role in her life. What were some of her attributes that created that bond?

CHAPTER ELEVEN

Jim

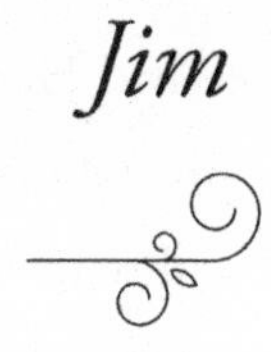

There is nothing wrong with grief; it's a healthy & sane response to loss. We have to start with telling the truth.

—Megan Devine

I had just undergone a procedure called an AV node ablation. It was supposed to control my heart rate due to atrial fibrillation. That way I wouldn't have to take those wretched beta blockers that depressed me. My daughter, Katy, had flown in from New York to accompany me. I was coming out of the anesthesia when I heard a gentle knock on the door in Cardiac Care.

"May I come in?" Katy appeared somewhat solemn as she sat on my bed, staring at me with compassion and concern. Something was awry.

"I have some sad news," she said.

"Oh my, someone close to us has died," I blurted in my semi-conscious state.

"It's Uncle Jim. He died in his sleep while in Hawaii on vacation. Cici did CPR while she and Charlie anxiously awaited the ambulance, but the medics were not able to revive him."

My brother, Jim, 83, was in Hawaii to celebrate Easter with his wife, Charlie, and daughter, Cici, and her family. That day he had stood with Cici and her husband, Fred, watching the sun set as his grandson, Chase, scurried up and down the beach, blowing soap bubbles. Then Jim played 18 holes of golf, shooting an 83. That evening, he and Chase assembled their clothes for their visit to the Pearl Harbor National Memorial. Jim had told his grandson about this pivotal moment in US history—Japan's attack on Pearl Harbor, and the subsequent entry of the United States into World War II.

As I clung to my rosary, praying for the soul of my departed brother, I reflected on my last time with him. How does one grieve the loss of a sibling who one never really knew until his life took a dramatic turn in his final years?

Pulling back the curtain on our lives, I endeavored to tie together the loose ends in my relationship with my brother. Our classic sibling rivalry, complicated by our mother's illness, included taunts about my weight, and legions of barbs and putdowns. Perhaps this was a way of controlling his life, for he couldn't control our mother's Parkinson's. So, he acted out his angst. It didn't help that my maiden aunts would lecture him every time he would sneak the car out against my father's will, stay out too late, or not come home with the right grades. Having a high-achieving father who expected his only son and namesake to excel in the classroom and on the sports field was a heavy burden to place on a vulnerable teen facing the loss of his mom.

As referenced in chapter two, Jim supported me, despite his challenges, when it came to getting my wish for a fourteenth birthday celebration. The party happened, and my mother was there, grace intact.

She died two years later. I had never seen Jim cry, but there we were, surrounding my mother's death bed as Jim's tears formed a puddle on her muslin sheets. Then we each went into our separate rooms without a word about the enormity of the loss we had just witnessed. I suspect that most of us had a separate meltdown. Mine involved going down the back stairwell to the kitchen and eating an entire angel food cake from Heinemann's Bakery in Evanston.

That was my way of seeking an island of calm. But it seemed that emotionally Jim had one foot on the accelerator and one on the brake. He used his bedroom wall and street lights as targets for his BB gun, while I cried, prayed, and ate chocolate chip cookies.

While my self-confidence diminished, my brother's popularity soared. I was known as "Jim Donnelly's little sister." My friends were eager to date him, but he would not fix me up with his friends. He convinced me that I was overweight and not a good conversationalist, so I didn't press the issue.

Once we got into college, however, things turned around. I gained self-confidence, thanks to the nuns at Barat College of the Sacred Heart, who were surrogate moms. I began entertaining, for our home was a perfect venue for parties. Over the holidays Jim and I would co-host one, inviting our friends from college. I was thrilled when one of Jim's friends, John McGowan, invited me to *his* party. John was president of his class at Loyola Academy and went on to Annapolis Naval Academy. My classmates yearned to have a date with him, especially when he wore his officer's uniform. I felt like I had won the Oscar when he asked me to his New Year's Eve party.

The best part of the event was at 12:00 a.m. when *Olde Lang Syne* rang out and the bells from St. Athanasius Church chimed. Wow! His friends were great kissers! There was a downside to that celebration, however. My brother had a Navy commission as a Lieutenant J.G. and was leaving for San Francisco because the Korean War was underway. I was terrified that he would be killed. That's when our relationship changed and softened.

I was a senior at Barat. Jim had gone to the University of Notre Dame and then received his commission at the Newport Officer Training School. That was a real coup for him. At Barat I always wore a medal of Mary, the Blessed Virgin. That was *my* commission. I wanted to give Jim something to keep him out of harm's way. As we sat on the steps of John McGowan's house on that first day of 1953, I handed him a scapular medal with Mary on one side and Jesus on the other. I told him that if he wore it at all times, he would come back safely. Sixty years later he reminded me of that medal, which I had forgotten about.

Jim *did* come back safely. He married Charlie, and I was the maid of honor. I moved to New York and forged my own life there. Then I headed to San Francisco and eventually returned to Chicago, married Ed, and we had two sons a year apart. The second, Thomas Aquinas, would be Jim's godson. Then Ed and I moved to Hartford, Connecticut, where our daughter, Katy, was born. Fast-forward eighteen years: Jim flew from Chicago to Hartford to attend Tom's graduation from prep school. Ed and I were in the midst of a divorce, and I told Jim that it would be a great gift, not only to Tom, but to our entire family, if he came to that graduation. He did. That not only turned around our relationship but also endeared Jim to all the children, especially Tom.

His generosity took other forms. When I lost my job after moving back to Chicago, he set up networking interviews with his influential friends. When I was rear-ended in an automobile accident on Michigan Avenue, Jim arranged for me to consult with the premier attorney handling accident claims. As a result, I was awarded a sum that gave me a much-needed financial cushion. And when I developed heart problems, he connected me with his cardiologist, who regularly reviewed my medical records and talked with my cardiologist prior to a heart procedure.

But there was one occasion that endeared him not only to me, but also to my children. When my former husband, Ed, died in Florida, Jim flew across the country, along with other family and friends, to attend the wake and funeral. He also served as a pallbearer. This was Jim's toast at the dinner after the funeral: "How many years have you been divorced?" he bellowed as the glasses clinked. "Thirty," was my response. "Here's to my sister, who has set an example for all of us." "Hear! Hear!"

Along with Jim's approval came a relationship that deepened as we aged. In the process we were able to eke some happiness from the loose ends of our lives. I found mine by coming to Seattle to be a Jesuit Volunteer. Jim found his by volunteering at the Betty Ford Clinic and the Coachella Mission for the poor. He taught his son Jamie's children how to play golf. And one received a golf scholarship to college because of the expertise she learned from him. I found myself in a tender, affectionate relationship with Jim for the last three years of his life. Part of that process was simply being honest with each other. I often swallowed my feelings when Jim offended me. But now I was confident enough to tell him how I felt.

A month had gone by since I sent Jim a Barnes & Noble gift certificate for his eightieth birthday. I asked him if he had received it.

"Oh, yeah, thanks a lot."

"Jim, it seems to me that I am always the one to initiate contact with you. And it hurts me when I send you a gift and you don't acknowledge it. Does it mean that you don't want to hear from me; that you don't care about the gift? My relationship with my siblings is important to me. We're at the end of our lives, and I don't know about you, but I cherish connections with you and Marie."

Jim responded, "You know, I'm so absorbed with the stress in my life, I'm not aware of how my behavior is affecting other people. You will be hearing from me on a regular basis."

This was the most emotionally authentic conversation I'd ever had with him. It was not about joking around; it was about how we felt. How sad that it took so long, but it was still a gift, albeit a late one.

The thin slice of life remaining to him was a rich and honest one. We spoke regularly. He shared the pain that he felt in never knowing our mother. The men in his support group often berated their moms, blaming the cluttered debris in their lives on them. He told them how lucky they were to have moms, and that they should work on their relationships with them before it was too late. "I never really knew my mom. She died when I was a teenager," he told them.

Jim wouldn't have revealed his feelings with such honesty unless he knew that they were safe with me and that I would be respectful of what he shared. As a result, our weekly conversations were some of the most honest, compassionate, and transformative exchanges I'd ever known with Jim. And to be authentic, these exchanges should have been mutual. That's why I regret that I did not share with him that I was going in for a heart procedure. He would have wanted to know. But I intended to tell him the outcome when I was discharged from the hospital. That was the day Jim died.

The news of Jim's death spread throughout the Coachella Valley, where he lived with his family and his Golden Retriever, Wrigley. Flags flew at half-mast at both PGA West and Skokie Country Club, where he played multiple rounds of golf with friends and family. People from all walks of life appeared at the warm California desert, where his funeral was held. Friends like Terrina, the PGA West security guard, who, on her day off, hand-delivered a bouquet of fresh flowers and a big hug, along with a card signed by the security staff. Bob, the pharmacist at Ralph's, who took such good care of Jim, made a special effort to be there. Each one of them, I'm sure, learned lessons of grace and compassion.

The intercessions at Jim's funeral were designed for him and written by his children and a multitude of nieces and nephews. Here are my favorites:

- In thanksgiving for Jim's generous spirit, zest for life, and for the ways he taught us to not take ourselves too seriously.
- For Jim's inexhaustible compassion, attentiveness, and fatherly wisdom, not only for his own children, but for his many nieces and nephews.

As I listened to them, I reflected that Jesus does not so much take away, but instead, transforms. Yes, Jim was transformed in his last years, but so was the world that surrounded him. That world is a better place because he was in it.

REFLECTION AND JOURNALING

Leaning into your grief and always erring on the side of expressing rather than inhibiting or ignoring your thoughts and feelings—will bring you to a place of transformation.

—Alan Worfelt

- What effect did Jim's mother's death have on his adolescence?
- What steps did Jim take as an adult to heal from this loss?
- Have you ever had a relationship with a family member or friend that was mended as a result of working through your differences? What did you learn from that experience?
- Did you have someone guide you through this time? Was that a counselor, family member, your faith community, or a counselor?
- It is never too late to ask for forgiveness. What do you suggest for those who are searching for ways to do so as they come close to the end of their lives?

CHAPTER TWELVE

Me

Then you must not grieve so sorely,

For I love you dearly still;

Try to look beyond earth's shadows,

Pray to trust our Father's will.

Excerpt from the poem *Safely Home*
—Author Unknown

My daughter is a New York City actor who just landed her first Broadway show. A United States premiere, it has changes to the script every day in rehearsal. She's been telling me you can always tell a great play; every scene is essential. Every scene moves the plot forward. Every story of grief that I have experienced has been a scene from the script of my life, propelling me forward to the final act.

I set out to write a narrative uncovering my long-buried trauma of childhood losses. As I delved into these stories, they tapped into a history of all of my other losses: a home, a marriage, a job, many dear relationships, and now my own health. This collection would not have been complete without acknowledging all of the fragments of loss. And yet, I do not view my life story as one of loss, but rather, one of **transformation, hope,** and **deepened spirituality**. In this—my final chapter—life is not an encyclopedia of lost stories, so much as a symphony of reasons to celebrate.

Transformation

The Catholic Church has always taught that the dignity that must be accorded to human life stems from a bottomless ability to transform ourselves—to be ever growing into something more, to embrace the power of transformation. One transformation came with my friend Jeanette's phone call twenty years ago, when I lived in Chicago. With excitement in her voice, she read me an advertisement in *America* magazine, announcing the creation of a Jesuit Volunteer ElderCorps in Seattle.

Jeanette said, "Helen, this is what you've been waiting for!"

Was this the call I'd been waiting for? Should I test the waters? Would I lose too much? It turns out not. I didn't lose my apartment overlooking Lake Michigan. I leased it. I put my furniture in storage, gave most of my wardrobe to women's shelters, sold my car, and headed for Seattle to work on behalf of Plymouth Housing, a non-profit recognized for its programs designed to bring stability to the lives of the homeless. I took an elderly woman suffering from depression to her first symphony ever. I shopped for furniture for those getting their first homes. I accompanied a terrified Native American woman to the dentist to have a tooth pulled. When the year was over, I decided to remain in the Northwest for its brand of spirituality. The chance to create renewed hope for those who had lost everything—that made me feel found. Had I not embraced this opportunity, I would not have experienced this life-giving transformation.

Hope

At age 87, I *am* finding hope in Seattle, where I remain after twenty years. Yet, despite the fact that I was recently diagnosed with multiple myeloma—cancer of the bone marrow—I view these years as among my happiest. It seems contradictory that such a diagnosis should be one of hope, especially since I was just recovering from a major exacerbation of heart failure, but rather than diminish me, these experiences have given me a new lease on life.

Interestingly, I had been anxious about the possibility of having multiple myeloma since a routine blood test fifteen years ago revealed a predisposition to this disease. A bone marrow biopsy in May confirmed that I did have multiple myeloma and would need treatment. There is something comforting about knowing that a team of providers, family, and friends might be a source of personal transformation.

In the last few months there have been reassuring appointments with the palliative care doctor, the social worker, the nutritionist, the chaplain, the Myeloma Support Group, and the nurses in the Infusion Center. They all endeavored to make me well during this thin slice of life remaining to me and were prepared to help my family and me deal with challenges, as they arise.

And my kids gave me hope just by showing up. That's the best treatment imaginable.

My eldest son, Ed, came in from Toronto, Canada and was right there with me in the oncologist's office when the doctor gave us the grim news that the multiple myeloma was still active, despite aggressive chemotherapy. Added to that conversation was the doctor's response to my father's autopsy report revealing that he died of multiple myeloma. The doctor told me that my children and grandchildren "should be tested for the disease." Hearts heavy, Ed and I reentered my apartment, where I was greeted by my granddaughter Yutaka pleading for another *Curious George* story. She climbed up on my lap as we settled into her favorite chair and called out the colors and the numbers and giggled at George's antics. My heart lightened. Hopefully she'll remember me as the BaBa who taught her about that silly monkey.

My son Tom flew in from Pennsylvania after I took a tumble at the podiatrist's office. Tom watched me like a hawk. He accompanied me to sessions with the cardiologist, the palliative care doctor, and the social

Tom, Katy and Ed at my 80th birthday celebration.

worker, who listened to our sobering conversation about how I would spend my final days. He even slept on the living room floor so he was available if I needed him during the night. Tom also has much to celebrate, having just returned from his daughter Liana's White Coat ceremony at New York University. She hasn't chosen her specialty yet, but one thing is a given—it will be dedicated to serving the underprivileged.

There are also Katy's daily "Yay Prays" that come across my computer every morning. No longer than two minutes, a mini recording from her can be heard with a click. This has been a huge grace despite the geographic space between us. I've saved them all and reflect on them when I need a "pick me up." Today she read from Meister Eckhart, the twelfth-century German theologian. "If the only prayer you said was thank you that would be enough."

But there were more than “Yay Prays” from Katy. We had essentially “done all our work,” that arduous climb children and parents have the privilege of doing with each other in order to see how blessed their connection is. Some parents and children (maybe most, I fear), don’t get that chance. But Katy and I grabbed ours years ago. When the two of us sat down in front of the theater where she was performing one August evening in Seattle, she apologized for being “a jerky kid.” I reminded her that when she did that, she was, well, a teenager. We’ve been gleefully free of the bondage of mother/daughter drama ever since. According to Katy, that’s not the case with a lot of her friends and their mothers.

There are others who rallied around me. Sue, my late sister Peggy’s daughter and my goddaughter, cancelled plans to attend a family wedding in California so she could be with me as I recovered in the hospital from severe anemia and required three transfusions. My only remaining sibling, my dear sister Marie, age 95, accompanied by her son David, traveled from Annapolis, Maryland, to check out her little sister’s well-being. And my friend Carol spent four hours in the Emergency Room clasping my healthcare directives as I experienced the transfusions.

I am in awe over the reverence with which Ann, my Seattle friend and spiritual mentor, creates an altar on my dining room table or hospital tray when she brings me the Eucharist. When my neighbor Teri brought me Eucharist, it was often accompanied by bouquets of flowers. And I can count on a visit from my soulmate Peg, whether in Assisted Living or at the hospital. But the gift of gifts one Sunday afternoon was a visit from Father Mike Ryan, pastor of St. James Cathedral. He not only brought me the Eucharist but also anointed me with oils rubbed in the shape of a cross on my forehead, hands, and feet. I knew at that moment that my path to healing was underway.

Does spending most of my time at doctors' appointments, in emergency rooms and counseling sessions, in visits from friends and family, and getting blood transfusions further God's kingdom? When accompanied by folks like these, my answer is yes, indeed!

Deepened Spirituality

As I climb the ladder of years, I wonder if the essential aim of old age is to discover what matters most and to simply live a good life.

I think of a recent Mass at St. Ignatius Chapel at Seattle University, when I was touched by Father Pat Howell's homily on "Overturning Expectations." He said, "Our own spiritual journey is unpredictable. It's full of surprises. God is always chasing us down, nipping at our heels. Moments of spiritual transcendence may suddenly overwhelm us, just as suffering opens us up to the deepest sources of the self and exposes fresh soil for new growth." I think of my visits with my spiritual director—the cornerstone of self-discovery that informs me to this day. "We are called to liberation and freedom," she reminded me, urging me to focus on graces I received.

Among these graces, I think of the ministry of healing in my condo. When I walk out of the building door and witness the stark contrast between my inside and outside neighbors, my heart aches. My inside neighbors are educated and prosperous. My outside neighbors are illiterate, speak in jumbled voices, and sleep on benches and buses. This ache has motivated my neighbors and me to empty our storage bins and donate school supplies and backpacks to homeless youth. We make Thanksgiving dinner for residents at Plymouth Housing, and we furnished an apartment for St. Francis House, a non-profit that serves the poorest of the poor in Seattle.

It appears that a lot of my transformative work is ongoing, which begs these questions: How much time is remaining to me? What will take me? Does it really make that much difference when or how I die? The bigger questions are these: How have I lived? Do my children and grandchildren feel loved? Do they know how proud I am of them, not only for their accomplishments and their compassionate natures but also for their kindnesses to me as my life winds down?

Christian Wiman, author of *My Bright Abyss*, says that "we cannot imagine our own death until it is thrust upon us—that we live in a land where only other people die." Writing *Transformed by Grief: A Personal History* has not only helped me prepare for my own death but has also erased the image of the lone woman in Edward Hopper's painting *Automat.* That girl had no place to go. She reminds me of myself when living in New York in my twenties, so fragile, wondering what my future held.

During that time, I recalled how grief-stricken I was as a 16-year-old at my mother's graveside. With my father's arm around me, I heard the message, though it was unspoken: hold your head high, not low, for Mayor Daly is here. No tears.

But rummaging through my papers recently, I retrieved a tattered holy card from that very day, February 5, 1949, in a "Special Papers" envelope. The prayer hasn't changed, but I have. I invite you, dear reader, to reflect on this particular stanza about making sense of loss that is transformative:

"There is work still waiting for you—So you must not idly stand: Do it now, while life remains."

As I finish this book, I am grateful there is still work to do. Now this New York City girl of the 1950s can lower her head and uncork her tears; no one there is going to accuse her of letting down her family (or the Mayor). The tears of my youth were the tears of a teenager not ready to let go of her mother; they were the tears of a lost adolescent. Having looked grief in the face many times, I unashamedly let the tears burst forth like a geyser. The tears I shed now in my final act are tears of renewal and newfound peace. In celebrating life every day, I continue to be transformed by grief.

REFLECTION AND JOURNALING

There is work still waiting for you,

So you must not idle stand;

Do your work while life remaineth—

You shall rest in Jesus' land

Excerpt from the poem *Safely Home*

—Author Unknown

- Have you, or someone close to you, faced the prognosis of a terminal illness? Who was that person to you? Share ways that you accompanied him or her on their final journey.
- What kind of spiritual support did you or that friend/family member receive?
- If you were facing this by yourself, what resources would you tap into?
- How do you balance the tension of grieving and living? Does your spiritual life shape that balance?

PART III

THE JOURNEY CONTINUES

Resources to Inform Your Own Story

This collection is about loss, grief, and transformation. It has been a gift to write about my own journey, to participate in the final journeys of loved ones, and to listen to the grace-filled insights embedded in the stories of so many others. In the knowledge that awareness is ever available, what matters is not so much *when* one begins, but *that* one begins. Our own healing stories, and those of others, have a powerful capacity no matter how much time has passed between when we lost a loved one and when we become authors of the story.

I am pleased to suggest some masters of the craft whose path-breaking insights are sure to add depth to your own understanding—and the assurance that you are in good company:

- C. S. Lewis's *Surprised by Joy* was published in 1955. This famed Irish journalist and author writes of his mother's death when he was nine. In it he laments that all happiness vanished from their household. Nevertheless, this enormous loss eventually led him to a deep faith in God that ultimately led to his conversion to Christianity.
- Thomas Merton's *Seven Storey Mountain* was published in 1952. This renowned American Trappist monk, writer, poet, mystic, activist, and scholar of comparative religion writes poignantly of losing both his parents to illness by the time he was an adolescent.
- Pierre Teilhard de Chardin wrote *The Divine Milieu* in 1929, but his religious superiors would not approve its being published until 1960, after his death. In this book he encourages his reader always to seek the path of spiritual beauty no matter how dire one's circumstances.

- Frederick Buechner's *Telling Secrets, The Sacred Journey,* and *Now and Then* were published in 1991, 1982, and 1983, respectively. In these inspiring, yet sobering, writings this Presbyterian minister and theologian writes poignantly of his father's suicide, his daughter's anorexia, and other losses.

I also would be remiss to leave out contemporary writers whose personal essays on strength, vulnerability and resilience have affected me deeply and directly. Having been fortunate to study under Ann Lamott, I am impressed to this day with her writing on divorce, single parenting, and the path to a deeper connection to life. Joan Didion's *The Year of Magical Thinking* is a study in raw grace and humility in the face of death. These authors and those listed below are only a few of the many whose work can assure us that we are not alone and that our stories matter. I have included inspirational quotes for dialogue and journaling, and websites for those who are grieving and wish to hone their writing skills.

READING RESOURCES

This reading list is rich with sources to inspire conversations and inform personal journaling or group study. As with the representative quotes, the list suggests a range of ways to discover understanding and context.

Augustine, Saint. *Confessions.* One of the most prolific writers of Christian antiquity, Augustine of Hippo reflects on the deep sense of human weakness and burning desire for union with God. Moody Publishers (2007)

Bender, Sheila. *A New Theology: Turning to Poetry in a Time of Grief.* After the death of her son in a tragic accident, the author found solace in reading and writing poetry. Imago Press (2009)

Bernardin, Joseph Cardinal. *The Gift of Peace: Personal Reflections.* This beautiful testament to courage and acceptance was published soon after the Cardinal's death from pancreatic cancer. His moving reflections convey the peace he achieved as he confronted his diagnosis and created a ministry for other cancer patients of all religions. Doubleday (1997)

Buechner, Frederick. *The Eyes of the Heart: A Memoir of the Lost and Found.* An ordained Presbyterian minister and Pulitzer Prize nominee, Buechner describes one of a series of journeys he takes to make sense of this life and what lies beyond. HarperSanFrancisco (1999)

Bush, Ashley David. *Transcending Loss: Understanding the Lifelong Impact of Grief and How to Make it Meaningful. A* psychotherapist and grief counselor, the author interviewed 50 people whose losses occurred two to 40 years ago. Their stories confirm that there is no timeframe to grief. Penguin Group (1997)

Butler, Katy. *Knocking on Heaven's Door: The Path to a Better Way of Death.* This absorbing work chronicles the author's challenges of caring for aging parents and navigating the distance between quality and quantity of years. Scribner (2013)

Byock, Ira, MD. *Dying Well: Peace and Possibilities.* President of the American Academy of Hospice and Palliative Medicine, Dr. Byock provides a blueprint for patients asking themselves end-of-life questions. It is also a resource for families who search for guidance, context, and a map for meaningful conversations. Riverhead Books (1997)

Callanan, Maggie and Patricia Kelley. *Final Gifts: Understanding the Special Awareness, Needs, and Communications of the Dying.* These Hospice nurses craft stories of those they walked with through 20 years of tending to the dying. Simon & Schuster (1992)

DeSalvo, Louise. *Writing as a Way of Healing: How Telling Our Stories Transforms Our Lives.* A professor of English at New York City's Hunter College, the writer creates a roadmap of being present to pain and recording it honestly as a pathway to possibility. Beacon Press (1999)

Devine, Megan. *It's OK That You're Not OK: Meeting Grief and Loss in a Culture That Doesn't Understand.* The author addresses the loneliness of grief and ways to help a grieving friend. Sounds True (2017)

Didion, Joan. *The Year of Magical Thinking.* This gifted writer's heart-wrenching memoir of her husband's death and her daughter's illness is a testament to her fortitude as she confronts the role grief plays in healing from unimaginable losses. Alfred A. Knopf (2005)

Dowling, Kathleen Singh. *The Grace in Dying: How We Are Transformed Spiritually as We Die.* The author combines her experience as a hospice worker with transpersonal psychology and many spiritual traditions. She extends the Kübler-Ross tradition to include Chaos, Surrender, and Transcendence. HarperCollins (1998)

Edelman, Hope. *Motherless Daughters: The Legacy of Loss.* The author writes an inspiring and enlightening chronicle of the impact that the loss of a mother in childhood has on a young woman's development. DeCapo Press (2006)

Erikson, Erik H. *The Life Cycle Completed.* As a pioneer of the concept of the identity crisis, this famed developmental psychologist contended that maturity is not the end of psychological growth. W. W. Norton & Co. (1982)

Farnsworth, Elizabeth. *A Train through Time: A Life, Real and Imagined.* This noted journalist and filmmaker confronts the impact that the death of her mother, when Elizabeth was nine, had on the course her professional life has taken. COUNTERPOINT (2017)

Fischer, Kathleen. *Winter Grace: Spirituality and Aging.* These reflections highlight the riches and possibilities of life's final stages and are promising to anyone facing their senior years. Upper Room Books (1998)

Hickman, Martha Whitmore. *Healing After Loss: Daily Meditations for Working through Grief.* These daily meditations to help the writer cope with the death of her 16-year-old daughter are sobering and comforting. HarperCollins Books (1994)

Kübler-Ross, Elisabeth. *On Death and Dying: What the Dying Have to Teach Doctors, Nurses, Clergy and Their Own Families.* At the University of Chicago Hospital this psychiatrist and pioneer in near-death studies explores how the terminal patient can serve as a teacher to all involved in his/her care. Scribner (1975)

Lewis, C. S. *A Grief Observed.* This famed philosopher's lament over the loss of his beloved wife, who passed away only four years after their wedding, is poignant and heart-wrenching. Seabury Press (1963)

Lewis, C. S. *Surprised by Joy: The Shape of my Early Life.* Considered this author's spiritual autobiography, it recaptures the Christianity he lost in his childhood. HarperCollins Publishers (1955)

Lindberg, Mary. *The Graceful Exit: A Pastor's Journey from Good-bye to Hello.* A Lutheran pastor helps clergy face the process of grieving when they leave their congregations and move to new pastoral calls. Alban Institute (2013)

Luke, Helen M. *Old Age: Journey into Simplicity.* This collection of essays on transforming aging and suffering shines a contemporary light on works by T. S. Eliot, William Shakespeare, and more. MorningLight Press (1987)

Nouwen, Henri J. M. *A Sorrow Shared.* A combined edition of *In Memoriam* and *A Letter of Consolation* was written on the occasion of this eminent Dutch theologian's mother's death. The first is to his mother. Ave Maria Press (1982) The second is Nouwen's effort to bring comfort to his father. HarperCollins (1982)

Rosenblatt, Roger. *Making Toast: A Family Story.* This is a lovely memoir (which he never wanted to write) by this noted author of six Off-Broadway plays and 15 books. The process helps him work through losing his daughter and building a new family. HarperCollins (2010)

Rosenblatt, Roger. *Kayak Morning: Reflections on Love, Grief, and Small Boats.* The author chronicles his life after his daughter's death and offers a personal meditation on grief itself. HarperCollins (2012)

Simmons, Philip. *Learning to Fall: The Blessings of an Imperfect Life.* This is a sobering record of a young man's response to an ALS (Lou Gehrig's disease) diagnosis. A professor of literature at Lake Forest College in Illinois, Simmons shares his search for peace throughout the nine years following his diagnosis. Bantam Books (2002)

Schewe, Beryl. *Habits of Resilience: Learning to Live Fully in the Midst of Loss.* A guide for caregivers and families, this practical, yet compassionate book is intertwined with tender stories. There is also a workbook with practices and reflections by this gifted chaplain and director of pastoral care. Twenty-Third Publications (2015)

Smith, Rodney. *Lessons from the Dying.* A Hospice worker and teacher of Vipassana meditation, Smith weaves stories of those facing death and includes reflections and exercises at the end of each chapter. Simon & Schuster (1998)

Sullender, R. Scott. *Losses in Later Life: A New Way of Walking with God.* A Presbyterian minister and counselor explores how the challenges of later life can lead to a time of spiritual growth. Haworth Pastoral Press (1989)

Teilhard de Chardin, Pierre, S.J. *The Divine Milieu.* Explores how salvation is discovered by embracing the world, rather than abandoning it. William Collins Sons & Co. Ltd., London (1960)

Wiederkehr, Macrina. *Seasons of Your Heart.* A Benedictine nun (O.S.B.) and member of St. Scholastica Monastery in Fort Smith, Arkansas, weaves inspiring daily reflections/prayers around the liturgical seasons. HarperCollins (1991)

INSPIRATIONAL QUOTES FOR DIALOGUE AND JOURNALING

The reassuring power of inspirational quotes cannot be underestimated, whether informing individual study or the work of spiritual directors and groups focused on loss or bereavement. The quotes below are given here to support that process, as are the reading resources and links that follow them.

"There is nothing wrong with grief; it's a healthy & sane response to loss. We have to start with telling the truth." Megan Devine, grief therapist. *It's OK That You're NOT OK.* Sounds True (2017)

"In the face of events that threaten to overwhelm our lives, storytelling gives us a way of reclaiming ourselves and reaffirming our connections with other people—those who listen to our stories and, by doing so, bear witness with us." Victoria Alexander, *In the Wake of Suicide: Stories of People Left B›ind.* Goodreads (1998)

"A child can live with anything as long as he or she is told the truth and is allowed to share with loved ones the natural feelings people have when they are suffering." Eda LeShan, psychologist and family counselor. *Learning to Say Good-bye.* Avon Books (1978)

"There is something you must always remember. You are braver than you believe, stronger than you seem, and smarter than you think." A. A. Milne, *Winnie the Pooh.* AbeBooks (1926)

"He knew he would never mail the letters, but he hoped the letters would help him release some of the emotions that churned around inside of him, an important step to his letting go." Lutheran Minister and Pastor Reverend Mary C. Lindberg, *The Graceful Exit: A Pastor's Journey from Good-bye to Hello*. Alban Institute (2013)

"Leaning into your grief and always erring on the side of expressing rather than inhibiting or ignoring your thoughts and feelings—will bring you to a place of transformation." Alan Worfelt, grief counselor and Director of Center for Loss and Life Transition. https://www.centerforloss.com

"You will lose someone you can't live without, and your heart will be broken, and the bad news is that you never completely get over the loss. But this is also the good news. They live forever in your broken heart that doesn't seal back up. And you come through." Anne Lamott, American novelist and non-fiction writer. *Traveling Mercies*. Anchor Books (1999)

"In our sleep, pain that cannot forget falls drop by drop upon the heart and in our despair, against our will, comes wisdom from the awful grace of God." *Agamemnon*, the first of the three tragedies comprising "The Oresteia" by ancient Greek playwright Aeschylus. SMK Books (2018)

"Only people who are capable of loving strongly can also suffer great sorrow, but this same necessity of loving serves to counteract their grief and heals them." Leo Tolstoy, twentieth-century Russian writer and recipient of the Nobel Prize in Literature. *Childhood*. 1886 Isabel F. Hapgood translation published by Thomas Y. Crowell & Co.

"When your fear touches someone's pain, it becomes pity; when your love touches someone's pain, it becomes compassion." Stephen Levine, American poet and author known for his writings on death and dying as influenced by Theravada Buddhism. *Unattended Sorrow: Recovering from Loss and Reviving the Heart.* Rodale Inc. (2005)

"And we wept that one so lovely should have a life so brief." William Cullen Bryant, nineteenth-century American Romantic poet. "Death of the Flowers." Yale University Press (1912)

"When we can talk about our feelings, they become less overwhelming, less upsetting, and less scary. The people we trust with that important talk can help us know that we are not alone." Fred Rogers, *Mr. Rogers' Neighborhood: Important Things to Remember.* Hatchett Books (2003)

"The reality is that we don't forget, move on, and have closure, but rather we honor, we remember, and incorporate our deceased children and siblings into our lives in a new way." Harriet Schiff, *The Bereaved Parent.* Crown Publishers (1977)

"What we have once enjoyed deeply we can never lose. All that we love deeply becomes a part of us." Helen Keller, the American author who was the first deaf and blind person to earn a college degree. *The World I Live In.* CreateSpace Publishers (1910)

"When a person is born we rejoice, and when they're married we jubilate, but when they die we try to pretend nothing has happened." Margaret Mead, American cultural anthropologist. Excerpt from "Understanding Grief," *Psychology Today* (August 3, 2016)

"No one ever told me that grief felt so much like fear." C. S. Lewis, *A Grief Observed.* The Seabury Press, Inc. (1963)

"Grief is not a disorder, a disease or a sign of weakness. It is an emotional, physical and spiritual necessity, the price you pay for love. The only cure for grief is to grieve." Earl Grollman, Rabbi, Beth El Temple, Boston, MA. Pioneer in crisis intervention. Beacon Press (1995)

"Grieving is as natural as crying when you are hurt, sleeping when you are tired or sneezing when your nose itches. It is nature's way of healing a broken heart." Doug Manning, pastor, author and grief counselor. *Don't Take My Grief Away from Me.* In-Sight Books, Inc. (1979)

"There is no grief like the grief which does not speak." Henry Wadsworth Longfellow, nineteenth-century American poet and educator. *The Prose Works of Henry Wadsworth Longfellow.* Hyperion and Kavanagh, Volume II, Houghton, Mifflin and Co. (1889)

"Grieving is a journey that teaches us how to love in a new way now that our loved one is no longer with us." Tom Attig, grief counselor. *Heart of Grief: Death and the Search for Lasting Love.* Oxford University Press (2000)

"Give sorrow words; the grief that does not speak whispers the o'er-fraught heart and bids it break." William Shakespeare, *Macbeth.* Riverhead Books (1998)

"Man, when he does not grieve, hardly exists." Antonio Porchia, Italian-born Argentinian writer of *Voces.* Copper Canyon Press (1943)

"For if sorrow is suppressed too much, it easily becomes worse." Moliere, seventeenth-century French satirist: *The Dramatic Works of Moliere.* Rendered into English by Henri Van Laun. G. Barrie (1875)

"She was no longer wrestling with the grief but could sit down with it as a lasting companion and make it a sharer in her thoughts." George Eliot (pen name of nineteenth-century English author Mary Ann Evans) *Middlemarch: A Study of a Provincial Life.* William Blackwood and Sons (1895)

"To lose track of our stories is to be profoundly impoverished, not only humanly, but also spiritually." Frederick Buechner, Presbyterian minister and theologian. *Telling Secrets.* HarperCollins Publishers (1991)

"As we teach our children to share, walk, and read, so should we teach them to cope with loss and grief, as these are a necessary part of life." Maggie Callanan, Hospice nurse, *Final Gifts.* Simon & Schuster (1992)

"When a mother dies too young, something inside her daughter always feels incomplete. There's a missing piece she continues to look for, an emptiness she keeps trying to fill." Hope Edelman, *Motherless Daughters.* DeCapo Press (2006)

"I found the process transformative. I was convinced I wouldn't survive it, but I did. Surprisingly, I was grateful for grief." Kate Goehring

"Tread softly because you tread on my dreams." William Butler Yeats. Irish poet, dramatist, and prose writer, and recipient of the Nobel Prize for Literature in 1923. *The Poems of W.B. Yeats: A New Edition.* Macmillan Publishing Co. (1983)

"Hello, sun in my face. Hello, you who made the morning and spread it over the fields. . . . Watch, now, how I start the day in happiness, in kindness." Mary Oliver, "*Why I Wake Early*": *MARY OLIVER DEVOTIONS.* Random House (2017)

"What is important for us to recognize is that Mother's own life invites us to see her death as a death that can bring us not only grief, but also joy, not only pain, but also healing, not only the experience of having lost but also the experience of having found." Henri J. M. Nouwen, *A Letter of Consolation.* Harper Collins (1982)

"Through his death our death is transformed from a totally absurd end of all that gives life its meaning into an event that liberates us and those whom we love." Henri J. M. Nouwen, *In Memoriam.* Ave Maria Press (1982)

"My friends are my estate. Forgive me then the avarice to hoard them." Emily Dickinson, *The Letters of Emily Dickinson.* Dover Books on Literature and Drama (2011)

"You must not grieve so sorely, for I love you dearly still; Try to look beyond earth's shadows; Pray to trust our Father's will." Author unknown

"There is work still waiting for you. . . . So you must not idly stand: Do it now, while life remains." Author Unknown

"You will always be part of me, for you were present through so much of my unfolding." Macrina Wiederkehr, Benedictine nun (O.S.B.) *Seasons of Your Heart.* Harper Collins (1991)

WEBSITES FOR THOSE WHO ARE GRIEVING

These websites and links to online articles offer just a few of the many online sources of inspiration for thinking about grieving, writing or both. As above, all can inform individual study, as well as work by spiritual directors or groups focused on loss or bereavement.

Journey Program (Grief and Loss) at Seattle Children's Hospital: Helps families who have experienced the death of a child cope with their loss and begin the grieving process.
http://www.seattlechildrens.org/clinics-programs/grief-and-loss

Camp Erin: Largest national bereavement program for youth grieving the death of a significant person in their lives. It provides three-day retreats for children ages 6-17 across the USA and Canada.
http://www.moyerfoundation.org/programs/CampErin_About.aspx

CLIMB (Children's Lives Include Moments of Bravery) Program
Provides emotional support for children, ages 6 to 11, who have a parent or primary caregiver with cancer. It is free and offered by the Swedish Cancer Institute in Seattle to the community-at-large. Contact Danielle McLaughlin at 425-313-4224.

National Widowers Support Groups: A place to learn how men grieve and connect with other widowers online or in a local support group.
https://nationalwidowers.org/support-groups

Hope Edelman: Offers resources for women who lost their mothers during childhood or adolescence. Beginning with the author's first book, *Motherless Daughters*, this website includes 60 Motherless Daughter support groups, as well as retreats, and videos.
http://hopeedelman.com/

St. Vincent DePaul Catholic Church, Omaha, Nebraska: Provides Bereavement Companions whereby a parishioner accompanies one through the first year of grief. The bereaved one receives monthly messages, prayers, reflections, phone calls, and cards.
https://www.svdpomaha.org/parish-outreach/care-and-compassion-ministry/grief-support

Center for Grief Recovery and Therapeutic Services, Chicago, Illinois: Helps the bereaved heal from grief and grow into a more grounded and vital life. Includes therapy and programs on sudden death in the workplace.
https://griefcounselor.org/resources/helpful-websites

GriefShare Offers seminars to help one recover from loss. These groups meet throughout the US, Canada, and 10 other countries. For the first year one receives an encouraging email message each day.
http://www.griefshare.org/

Hospice Foundation Support-Groups: Provides grief support groups that are open to those who didn't use Hospice services. Funeral homes, hospitals, and places of worship are excellent resources. Includes a monthly newsletter with practical advice for people coping with loss and bereavement.
http://hospicefoundation.org/Grief-(1)/Support Groups

Grief Recovery Method: An action-based group that offers reading and writing assignments for those recovering from loss. Involves an eight-week format in a group or individual setting, facilitated by Grief Recovery Method Specialists.
http://www.griefrecoverymethod.com/our-programs/support-groups

ARTICLES SHINING A LIGHT ON THE PROCESS

Los Angeles Times writer Sandy Banks, whose mother died of cancer when Sandy was 19, reflects on the benefit of Hope Edelman's Motherless Daughters series.
http://www.latimes.com/local/la-me-banks-motherless-daughters-20140503-column.html

Warren Black, pastor *emeritus* of Oxford University United Methodist Church, interviews Frederick Buechner to thank him for his hope, his courage, and his honesty as reflected in his writings. That interview is published in this issue of *Sojourners*.
http://sojo.net/articles/reflections-loss-thanks-frederick-buechner

Ignatian Spirituality offers ways to grow in one's prayer life while living in a season of loss.
http://www.ignatianspirituality.com/prayer-while-grieving

Father Ron Rolheiser, noted theologian and spiritual writer, reflects on loss, grief, and obsessions, sharing insights from renowned psychologist Antoine Vergate and paleontologist Pierre Teilhard de Chardin, S.J.
http://www.ronrolheiser.com/dealing-with-loss-grief-and-obsessions

Journalist Judith Valente writes of her connection with Kathleen Norris, noted poet and non-fiction writer, and reflects on how Norris has helped family members experience a good death. A Benedictine oblate, Norris also shares the challenges that depression has presented for her and her family.
http://www.americamagazine.org/content/dispatches/writing-death-and-monastic-wisdom-conversation-kathleen-norris

PLACE-BASED WRITING RESOURCES

To remind readers and service providers that rich opportunities for writing and coming together likely exist in their own backyards, I offer the following resources in Seattle and New York. Doubtless, similar opportunities exist in countless local communities nationwide.

Seattle

Hedgebrook Farms is a literary nonprofit that supports visionary women writers. Located in Langley, WA
https://www.hedgebrook.org/

Hugo House is a writing center that offers readings, classes, and consultations with professional writers.
https://www.hugohouse.org/classes/course-catalog/

The Seattle Public Library provides year-round writing circles and a fall series of 20 classes focused on the craft of writing.
https://www.spl.org/programs-and-services/learning/seattle-writes

The Writers' Workshop offers a wide variety of writing classes in Seattle, Europe, and online.
https://www.thecreativewritersworkshop.com/memoir-writing-course-online/

New York

The Gotham Writers Conference offers courses for adults and teens, as well as writing opportunities beyond its classes. These classes are also available online.
https://www.writingclasses.com/?utm_source=bingads&utm_medium=cpc&utm_term=gotham+writers

The Write Life lists 47 writers' retreats located throughout the world. They offer a combination of workshops, tours, and interaction with a small group of writers.
https://thewritelife.com/writing-retreats/

Online Classes

The New School has online writing classes that are accessible and convenient, and have a wide range of resources and learning options.
https://www.newschool.edu/writing

The National Association of Memoir Writers provides a framework for writing a memoir, the foundation of learning the craft. Some resources are free and some are available to those ready to commit to a more in-depth process.
https://namw.org

THE HEALING POWER OF POETRY AND PRAYER

Beloved poet William Carlos Williams famously observed that "it is difficult to get the news from poems . . . yet men die miserably every day for lack of what is found there." With that enduring observation in mind, the poetry and prayers below have helped me and countless others find reassurance and so much more, when other words have failed.

A Summer Day

Who made the world?
Who made the swan, and the black bear?
Who made the grasshopper?
This grasshopper, I mean—
the one who has flung herself out of the grass,
the one who is eating sugar out of my hand,
who is moving her jaws back and forth instead of up and down—
who is gazing around with her enormous and complicated eyes.
Now she lifts her pale forearms and thoroughly washes her face.
Now she snaps her wings open, and floats away.
I don't know exactly what a prayer is.
I do know how to pay attention, how to fall down
into the grass, how to kneel in the grass,
how to be idle and blessed, how to stroll through the fields,
which is what I have been doing all day.
Tell me, what else should I have done?
Doesn't everything die at last, and too soon?
Tell me, what is it you plan to do
With your one wild and precious life?

—Mary Oliver

The Layers

I have walked through many lives, some of them my own,
and I am not who I was,
though some principle of being
abides, from which I struggle
not to stray.
When I look behind,
as I am compelled to look
before I can gather strength
to proceed on my journey,
I see the milestones dwindling
toward the horizon
and the slow fires trailing
from the abandoned camp-sites,
over which scavenger angels
wheel on heavy wings.
Oh, I have made myself a tribe
out of my true affections,
and my tribe is scattered!
How shall the heart be reconciled
to its feast of losses?
In a rising wind
the manic dust of my friends,
those who fell along the way,
bitterly stings my face.
Yet I turn, I turn,
exulting somewhat,
with my will intact to go
wherever I need to go,

and every stone on the road
precious to me.
In my darkest night,
when the moon was covered
and I roamed through wreckage,
a nimbus-clouded voice
directed me:
"Live in the layers,
not on the litter."
Though I lack the art
to decipher it,
no doubt the next chapter
in my book of transformations
is already written.
I am not done with my changes.

—Stanley Kunitz

The Writer

In her room at the prow of the house
Where light breaks, and the windows are tossed with linden,
My daughter is writing a story.

I pause in the stairwell, hearing
From her shut door a commotion of typewriter-keys
Like a chain hauled over a gunwale.

Young as she is, the stuff
Of her life is a great cargo, and some of it heavy:
I wish her a lucky passage.

But now it is she who pauses,
As if to reject my thought and its easy figure.
A stillness greatens, in which

The whole house seems to be thinking,
And then she is at it again with a bunched clamor
Of strokes, and again is silent.

I remember the dazed starling
Which was trapped in that very room, two years ago;
How we stole in, lifted a sash

And retreated, not to affright it;
And how for a helpless hour, through the crack of the door,
We watched the sleek, wild, dark

And iridescent creature
Batter against the brilliance, drop like a glove
To the hard floor, or the desk-top,

And wait then, humped and bloody,
For the wits to try it again; and how our spirits
Rose when, suddenly sure,

It lifted off from a chair-back,
Beating a smooth course for the right window
And clearing the sill of the world.

It is always a matter, my darling,
Of life or death, as I had forgotten. I wish
What I wished you before, but harder.

—Richard Wilbur, *Bottom of Form*

Gates of Prayer

We Remember Them…

In the rising of the sun and in its going down,
We remember them;
In the blowing of the wind and in the chill of winter,
We remember them;

In the opening of buds and in the warmth of summer,
We remember them;
In the rustling of leaves and the beauty of autumn,
We remember them;
In the beginning of the year and when it ends,
We remember them;

When we are weary and in need of strength,
We remember them;
When we are lost and sick at heart,
We remember them;
When we have joys we yearn to share,
We remember them;
So long as we live, they too shall live
For they are now a part of us as
We remember them.

—Judaism Prayer Book

Face to Face

Day after day, O lord of my life,
shall I stand before thee face to face.
With folded hands, O lord of all worlds,
shall I stand before thee face to face.

Under thy great sky in solitude and silence,
with humble heart shall I stand before thee face to face.

In this laborious world of thine, tumultuous with toil
and with struggle, among hurrying crowds
shall I stand before thee face to face.

And when my work shall be done in this world,
O King of kings, alone and speechless
shall I stand before thee face to face.

—Rabindranath Tagore

Aging/Dying

When the signs of age begin to mark my body
(and still more when they touch my mind);
When the ill that is to diminish me or carry me off
Strikes from without or is born within me;
When the painful moment comes
In which I suddenly awaken
To the fact that I am ill or growing old;
And above all at that last moment
When I feel I am losing hold of myself
And am absolutely passive within the hands
of the great unknown forces that have formed me;
in all those dark moments, O God,
grant that I may understand that it is you
(provided my faith is strong enough)
Who are painfully parting the fibers of my being
In order to penetrate to the very marrow
Of my substance and bear me away within yourself.

—Pierre Teilhard de Chardin, S.J.

ABOUT THE AUTHOR

Helen Donnelly Goehring is a Seattle-based writer and a retired Development Director for nonprofits. Her development career spans over three decades of fundraising in Connecticut, Illinois, and Washington. In Hartford, Connecticut, she increased support for independent schools, social service agencies, and one of the nation's oldest and largest psychiatric hospitals. In Chicago her work included raising funds for at-risk children and youth in vulnerable communities. She finished her career in Seattle after completing her Jesuit Volunteer ElderCorps year, building an endowment for seniors who had depleted their resources.

Her writing has appeared in a range of local and national newspapers and magazines, including opinion pieces advocating improved mental health, education, and assistance programs for the homeless. Below are selected writings:

- *America Media* (March 7, 2018)*:* "Yes to All That: My Jesuit Volunteer ElderCorps Call"
- "Pray the Bells Toll Less in 2018 for our Homeless Neighbors"—A *Seattle Times* op-ed on the plight of the homeless in Seattle. November 18, 2017.
- "Taking Notes—an Assisted Life" (2013): This piece won second place in the *Writing It Real* competition published by Sheila Bender, noted Northwest author whose own writing chronicles how reading and writing poetry helped her cope after the loss of her 25-year-old son. WritingItReal.com is Ms. Bender's instructional magazine.
- *In Your Midst* (December 2017, December 2016, March 2006, and August 2008): This bi-annual magazine, published by St. James Cathedral, the cathedral for the Catholic Archdiocese of Seattle,

featured her piece "Discovering Compassion on the #2 Bus" in its December 2017 issue (pages 10–11). This was a feature article. The others were one-page articles.

- *Focus on Philanthropy* (2008–2014): Helen created and wrote this online and in-print journal as Horizon House's first philanthropic newsletter aimed at raising funds for elderly residents who have outlived their resources. Circulation: 1500. Horizon House is a continuing care retirement community in Seattle.
- Swedish Hospital Neuroscience Institute Newsletter (2016): Helen wrote this article relating her experience of undergoing brain surgery while grasping a rosary blessed by Pope Francis. https://www.swedish.org/~/media/Images/Swedish

A founding member of the Associates of the Religious of the Sacred Heart in Chicago and Seattle, Goehring regularly attends the Order's Children of Mary retreats and meetings. After twenty years she continues spiritual direction with a former faculty member of Seattle University's School of Theology and Ministry, where she audits classes. Goehring also serves on St. James Cathedral's Pastoral Vision Council.

She has three children: a son who is a professor of music history and Mozart scholar; another son who is a jazz trumpet player and composer, and a daughter who is an actor.

Made in the USA
Monee, IL
01 November 2020